TAKING THE BIBLE SERIOUSLY

TAKING THE

LEANDER E. KECK

BIBLE SERIOUSLY

A HADDAM
HOUSE
BOOK

ASSOCIATION PRESS • NEW YORK

TAKING THE BIBLE SERIOUSLY

Publisher's stock number: 1505

Library of Congress catalog card number: 62-16872

MANUFACTURED IN U. S. A.

to my parents

JACOB and ELIZABETH KECK

in whom
Jeremiah's promise
comes true:

I will put my Law within them
    and I will write it upon their hearts
And I will be their God
    and they shall be my people.

A WORD

ABOUT THIS BOOK

T HIS ESSAY ASSERTS that there is a way of reading the Bible which opens the door to vital faith without shutting the door to critical thought. The Bible is more revered than read because most people do not know how to read it with understanding; hence they don't read it at all. Consequently, it is the most neglected resource of our time. Even people who hail it as "the precious Word of God" often fail to catch its inner dynamic. True, reading the Bible can be a formidable undertaking; but it can also bring one into the presence of God. It can do this if we are willing to read it seriously.

Taking the Bible seriously involves more than simply reading it piously. On the one hand, it demands a willingness to listen openly to what the writer says about God's involvement with his creatures, and to his reasons for saying it as well. On the other hand, it requires the courage to deal with what he says, and to make an honest response to it. Moreover, taking the Bible seriously means that we do not know in advance just what kind of response we shall make. In fact, the seriousness of our reading can be measured by the extent to which we permit significant disagreement. It may be better to argue with the Bible than to shrug it off. In other words, this book maintains that we take the Bible seriously when we allow both the reader and the Bible to meet each other honestly. Such a meeting brings both opportunity and danger. The Bible risks being set aside by a person who cannot believe it, and the reader risks being convinced by what the Bible has to say. That is, if the reader takes the Bible seriously enough to meet its message, God himself may apprehend him. This essay explores the basis for reading the Bible thus and sketches its consequences.

The book invites readers who have difficulty in taking the Bible seriously to participate in considering certain basic issues. Not all important problems can be treated, of course; nor can any of them be discussed fully. This is not our purpose. Rather, this essay aims to help the reader think systematically for himself. Therefore we shall not try to soften debate but to elicit discussion. One way to participate is to fill the margins with comments. Another is to check the Bible itself from time to time. The biblical text is seldom quoted here, though references are scattered throughout. Reading these will give concreteness to the argument and raise a steady supply of questions as well. Besides, no book about the Bible is worth its weight in wastepaper if it does not lead one to read the Bible for himself. *Great — no substitute for the Bible*

This essay assumes that the Bible can speak for itself if it has a chance to do so. The Bible does not need to be kept in a back room where no embarrassing questions intrude. As a matter of fact, the real dynamic of the Bible usually lies dormant until we bring our basic questions to it. Its real power reveals itself when we take it seriously enough to learn what it has to say to our questions and to risk having our questions dealt with in unexpected ways. This approach requires going beyond reading it as a mere book; it asks that we read it so that writer and reader address one another. To facilitate this, we shall attempt to understand the Bible from within, as much as possible on its own terms. Moreover, this book does not mount the ramparts to defend the Bible against the onslaughts of the modern world; nor does the writer feel guilty for asking, even pressing, a modern reader's questions. To the contrary, such a relentless reading is necessary if the writer is to meet us where we really are. In this way we can discover the power of the Bible for vital faith today. Anyone who is looking for ammunition against such an approach ought to put this book down—unless he is willing to engage in a conversation.

A central theme is that the historical-critical method is an indispensable tool for anyone who wants to know what the Bible says. Fortunately, today one does not need to defend the use of this method for studying the Bible because in some form it has been accepted on all sides. Unfortunately, however, the religious and theological consequences of this method often remain undrawn, if not actually denied. For example, students are sometimes told that studying the Bible critically will not affect their faith because the course-work is concerned only with the "facts" about the biblical documents. Such a position is quite misleading and is mostly nonsense. Unless the Bible is irrelevant to faith in the first place, a particular way of studying it inevitably affects the understanding of the Bible, and hence what one believes. Only a faith without any content can remain unaffected. Hence, this book outlines some of the ways scholarly work affects the authority of the Bible for faith.

Some readers may shy away from a somewhat complex approach to the Bible. They may put this book down with a wistful desire that things might be simple again, that one could settle the matter by announcing boldly, "Either you believe it or you don't." There is a place for such a basic decision, but it is not at the outset when one begins systematic reflection about the Bible. Such simplicity is an achievement, not a refuge. Rather, because the Bible emerged as men wrestled with issues which embarrassed their faith as well as they supported it, the Bible is usually more prepared to face tough problems than its readers. In fact, this is one reason it is worth taking seriously.

Finally, without shifting responsibility, I should like to express a word of appreciation publicly, especially since the book largely omits that fetish

of the academic world, the footnote. My obligations to unmentioned literature will be apparent
to seasoned readers. In addition, fellow students
of the Bible have sharpened my thinking. Some
of these have been my classmates, some were my
students at Wellesley College and at Vanderbilt,
others my associates in both schools. Two col-
leagues at Vanderbilt, Professors Gordon Kauf-
man and James Sellers, read the manuscript at
different stages and made valuable comments.
My wife contributed disarming questions and
steadying encouragement; both have been indispensable. But especially important contribu-
tions have come from my teachers of the Bible;
the list begins with my parents, to whom this
volume is dedicated with gratitude.

Unless otherwise indicated, the scriptural quotations in this book are from the Revised Standard Version of the Bible, copyrighted 1946 and
1952 by the Division of Christian Education, National Council of Churches.

LEANDER E. KECK
THE DIVINITY SCHOOL
VANDERBILT UNIVERSITY
NASHVILLE, TENNESSEE

CONTENTS

13]

THE BIBLE
IS A PROBLEM

THERE IS NO NEED to argue that many people find the Bible to be a problem. The fact that year after year it manages to top the best-seller list hides the fact that most readers have serious difficulties with it. Much more significant than the sales record would be a report of how many of these Bibles were actually read with comprehension. Still more decisive might be knowing what kind of impact such reading might have had, for it is possible to understand the Bible without believing it. In any case, people tend to respect the Bible even if they do not know what to make of it. The aim of this chapter, then, is not to demonstrate the fact that we have problems with the Bible but to bring certain of these difficulties into focus.

Why Can't I Understand It?

"If God spare my life, ere many years I will cause a boy that driveth the plough shall know more of the Scripture than thou dost." So spoke

15]

William Tyndale in 1522 as he set about providing a Bible every Englishman could understand.
The translation cost him his life. The irony is
that today, with dozens of English translations
available, the average English-speaking person
still does not understand the Bible.

For one thing, we have trouble with its language. This is especially true for those who continue to read the King James Version of 1611.
But even the flood of modern translations and
paraphrases have not solved the problem entirely. The reader meets strange phrases made up
of ordinary words which are combined to read
almost like a secret code—phrases like . . . the Son
of Man (what son of what man, and why all the
capitals?) . . . the prince of the power of the air
. . . walk by the Spirit. Translators keep such
phrases because they believe accuracy requires
them.

It does little good to say that such phrases are
metaphors, because, although this is true, it is
also obvious that we no longer understand what
such metaphors say. The metaphor has become
a cryptic cipher, and the language hides the
meaning instead of revealing it.

In the second place, we have trouble understanding the Bible because we live in a different
world. The things we take for granted, like the
"shape" of the universe, had not yet dawned on
the writers of the Bible; conversely, we treat the
things the writers took for granted, such as the
three-level universe or the influence of invisible
beings, as outmoded ideas which belong in the

museum together with witchcraft and alchemy. Thus, we hardly know what "the Spirit" is nor are we sure how to distinguish it from "the spirit"; nor do we understand what "the power of the air" is (certainly not air pressure or air power!) or why it should have a "prince." To say that this is a vivid metaphor for Satan merely restates the problem, for we do not know if we can believe in the existence of a personal evil being (Being?) at all. We may, of course, use the term "Satan" as a poetic personification of evil, but we still face the question of whether this is what the Bible intends to say. Similarly, we may continue to talk about God's being "up in heaven" because we remind ourselves, if we think of it at all, that this is figurative speech; actually we probably doubt if heaven is a place (or space-time entity of any sort) and we are not at all sure that it would be "up." But the biblical writers did not have such reservations, nor did they have to cross their fingers mentally when they wrote. They could answer the child's question, "Where is God?" more easily than we, for when even we say "He's everywhere" we may actually mean "He's *no-where*." Thus the more seriously we try to read the Bible on its own terms, the more aware we become that in a real sense it comes from another world.

There is still a deeper level on which we have difficulty: grasping what the Bible intends to say. Even if we determine the meanings the writer had in mind when he used a particular phrase, the very fact that we have to make an effort to

17]

see his point reveals that he no longer communicates directly. Thus we may learn that when Paul uses the phrase "walk in the Spirit" he is not talking about a kind of stride but a kind of life, a life impelled by divine power now resident within man. The more clearly we perceive what *Paul* understood by the term "Spirit" the more difficult it becomes *for us* to use it because we don't think in these terms any more. The term "spirit" has lost most of its content even though we still use the word "spiritual" to designate something intangible like loyalty or love. Yet it is one thing to say that we live by intangible relationships; it is something else to say we live by the Spirit because at least Paul was talking about more than a relationship—he was also talking about some*thing*. He never doubted that there was a realm of things, being, powers, or essences which were both intangible and real. So the question is forged: can we genuinely comprehend what Paul has to say?

Now we are at the heart of it. Let us assume that we understand what Paul was trying to say to his first readers; that is, we have succeeded in "breaking his code" and we are now able to listen in as he talks with his contemporaries. Our real problem now is whether Paul is worth listening to, whether he has anything to offer us today. We raise the question because we expect, perhaps because we have been taught to do so, that the Bible has something to say to us. After all, it's Scripture. In fact, this is precisely why the Bible poses the kind of problem it does.

What Difference Does It Make?

Our problems of understanding the Bible are serious because this book is Scripture; that is, a book with Godlike authority. This is true even in the so-called "post-Christian era" of today. The Bible has exerted formative influence on Western civilization. In fact, this culture cannot be understood without seeing the way the Bible has functioned as Scripture with divine authority, whether in the development of the Middle Ages, the Protestant Revolution, or certain elements of the resistance to totalitarianism. The Bible did not have authority because its contents have unique literary excellence (such a standard would exclude much of it) or because its teachings are the source of our pace-setting ideas (many of which are actually derived elsewhere). Rather, the Bible became a formative factor in our culture only because it became Scripture. That is, it became the basic authority for a community of faith, the Church, and through it for the culture as a whole. This is what we mean by "Scripture."

The picture comes into focus as we realize that the Bible is not the only Scripture mankind has. The Koran is the Scripture for Islam, and the Buddhist religion accords the Gitas high standing. The Communist faith has its Scripture also—the works of Karl Marx, Friederich Engels, and Nikolai Lenin. In each of these cultures, the Scriptures function as a pace-setting guide, even a court of appeal. At this point we are not concerned with the Bible's place among other Scriptures but simply with the point that our problems connected with the Bible are serious because they are the problems of our Scripture. They are the problems of not understanding clearly the nature and content of our religious norm.

We have similar problems understanding any ancient literature, whether it be the inscriptions on the pyramids or the Dead Sea Scrolls. But because these are not Scripture, the problem is primarily intellectual and not religious.

Moreover, it is largely the historians who have these problems because their work is to interpret the past. But Scripture is decisive for everyone. This is the reason Protestants, for whom the Bible has had unique and absolute authority, have been so active in translating and distributing the Bible in every place on earth. Since this Book is God's Word, they reason, every man must have it; if he cannot read it, he must be taught to read so that first of all he may read the Bible. Traditionally, the Scripture is God's Word for every man. This is why understanding it is so important.

But, as was suggested previously, the significant aspect of the problem involves more than understanding; it involves our ability to believe that the Bible has anything decisive to say to us today. In other words, can the Bible continue to be our Scripture? Can we still take it seriously enough for it to affect our lives and shape our culture? Or has the modern world made it both incomprehensible and unbelievable? This essay

[20

attempts to show how the Bible can still be Scripture in today's world.

This is not the only way the Bible may be read for religious purposes. Many people find it impossible to restrict themselves to one Scripture because they realize that all the sacred texts of mankind contain high ideals and worthwhile teachings. Hence, it is possible for each person to compile his own anthology of inspiration and precept. Even if this were to be published on India paper and bound in leather, this need not be a Scripture in the sense we have discussed. Rather, it would be a treasury of insight on which a person might draw from time to time. Such a volume might be spared many pages of our Bible which appear full of dull details and teachings of dubious merit. In place of such biblical gristle one might use the meatier contents of the Koran, the Gitas, and the teachings of Confucius. In this way, one might select the clearest insights of man. This is the rummage sale approach.

But it is premature. At least we question whether the compiler has understood the spectrum of mankind's Scriptures from within or whether he has merely combed them for those parts which appear to be useful. Without passing judgment on other Scriptures, we can say that this procedure shows an inadequate understanding of the Bible and of the kind of authority it may have. The Bible does have excellent passages which repeatedly inspire or alert the reader to a true sense of values, but to abstract them from their setting violates the very paragraphs the person admires. For example, I Corinthians 13 is the famous chapter on love. Though the beauty and depth of this passage are undeniable, interpreting it in terms of some sort of Love-idealism misses the point. The passage does not celebrate the glories of Love-with-a-capital-L. Instead, it points a pseudo-sophisticated group of Christians toward a life in which self-glorying is given up. When one sees the setting and the intent of the passage, he often stops admiring it because one's aesthetic appreciation *for* it is chastened by a sense of being judged *by* it.

On the other hand, the Bible also contains passages which appear to be useless and even objectionable, such as stories of vindictive palace revolts or offensive customs like executing an entire family for the offense of one man. But simply deleting them might also be a way of missing what the Bible can contribute. At least, one ought to ask why such stories were included, for perhaps the writers wanted to say something which is still worth hearing. Editing the Bible so that such materials no longer jar us may actually bypass important things the Bible can say to us.

The way to allow the Bible to have its say, without rejecting what we may learn from other Scriptures, is to let it continue to be *our Scripture*. Both words are important. The Bible can be *our* Scripture only if we are honest about the problems we have in reading it. This book intends to face such problems openly. The more the results of science and technology become ingrained in the outlook of our time, the more obscure and objectionable the Bible often seems. To be sure, there are many people for whom a sentence beginning "The Bible says . . ." carries an automatic mandate to believe it, more or less at face value. But, increasingly, such readers find themselves torn between their allegiance to the Bible as the Word of God and their understanding of the world in which they live. Moreover, these are not the only ones threatened by intellectual rupture. The more sophisticated reader also finds the impact of science (in virtually all disciplines) to be eroding confidence in the Bible. Students are sometimes uneasy with the current existentialist approach to the Bible because they sense that the issues of "Science and the Bible" have been swept under the rug. In any case, each generation must face the issues anew. There was a time when people believed that something was true simply because it was stated in the Bible; nowadays we want to know if what is in the Bible is true. All persons reading the Bible, regardless of their background, face this question in some form. Consequently, the kinds of problems raised by what the Bible says about the character of God or the world or his will for man must be faced openly, without fear or sense of guilt. In short, the Bible can be *our* Scripture insofar as we allow our real, modern selves to deal honestly with it.

Similarly, the Bible can be our *Scripture* only if we take it seriously enough to make an honest effort to understand it and to come to terms with

23]

it. In fact, one can measure its "Scripturehood" by the degree to which we are willing to risk hearing what the Bible actually has to say. As with any literature, the writer's message is larger than the mere content of what he says, for it includes what he is trying to communicate through what he writes. Only after seeing this underlying intent do we really know what the Bible wants to say. This is the proper point at which to decide what to do with it. Reading the Bible as Scripture requires allowing ourselves to be apprehended by what the writers have to say.

Our next task, then, is to see the character of the Bible as a whole (Chapter 2) and the tools for understanding such a Bible (Chapter 3). With this in mind, we can take up its central concerns (Chapters 4 and 5) and the kinds of issues they raise for us today (Chapters 6 through 8).

THIS KIND OF BIBLE

W E SHOULD NOT TAKE our kind of Scripture for granted. Even its structure shows that in contrast with Scriptures like the Book of Mormon, for instance, the Bible has a history. It is not a translation of secret writings on golden tablets as is claimed for the Mormon Scripture, nor did it fall from heaven as Islam asserts about the Koran. Seeing the kind of book the Bible is will sharpen the problems we face as we try to make sense of it.

Who's Responsible for Such a Book?

The Bible was not written as it now stands. The Table of Contents does not reveal the order in which the literature was written, nor is it an accurate guide to the authors. Our Bible is the result of collecting and editing a long series of writings. An important key to the Bible, then, lies in the purposes for which the literature was gathered together. This, in turn, leads us to the group which made the collection and first used it. The problem is complicated by the fact that the phrase "The Holy Bible" actually refers to

25]

three collections, to three Bibles. Therefore, when we ask "What Bible?" we ask "Whose Bible?" at the same time.

• The shortest collection is used by the Synagogue. It contains only the literature used by the Palestinian synagogues of the first century A.D.[1] When Jews speak of "The Bible" they refer to this collection which Christians call "The Old Testament." Long before the time of Christ it was translated from Hebrew into Greek by the Jewish community in Egypt. This Greek version,

[1] It is important to remember that first-century Palestinian Judaism was by no means unanimous in its judgment about what constituted the Bible. The opinion which prevailed, largely because other groups disappeared, was that of the Pharisees. Their Bible was our Old Testament, though in different order. Their bitter rivals, the Sadducees, accepted only the Pentateuch (the first five books of the Bible, commonly called The Books of Moses) as supreme authority. Since the Sadducees were largely identified with the Temple, they disappeared with its destruction; the Pharisees—being associated with the local centers of instruction and worship, the synagogues—survived to become the ancestors of Judaism as we know it today. The whole problem of what was Scripture in Palestinian Judaism during the time of Jesus has been reopened through the discovery of the so-called Dead Sea Scrolls.

These documents come from a group (commonly called Essenes) which opposed both Pharisees and Sadducees. They valued the same literature as is now in our Bible and wrote commentaries on it; however, they also prized other writings, many of which were not known before. The question is whether they thought as highly of this other material as they did of the biblical literature. A useful survey of what the caves have yielded is found in J. T. Milik, *Ten Years of Discovery in the Wilderness of Judaea,* John Strugnell, tr.—Studies in Biblical Theology No. 26 (Naperville, Ill.: Alec R. Allenson, Inc., 1959).

called the Septuagint because of the story that seventy men translated it, was also expanded to include additions to some books like Daniel and to include completely new ones like the so-called Wisdom of Solomon. This expanded Synagogue Bible served as the first Scripture of the early Church. Later, this enlarged edition of the Old Testament was translated into Latin and remains part of the Roman Catholic Bible today. The Protestant Reformers, however, accepted only the earlier Palestinian Bible and separated the additions into a subsidiary collection called "The Apocrypha," meaning literally "hidden away"— that is, withdrawn from official use. For years, Protestants printed the Apocrypha between the Old and New Testaments as "good and useful to read." It is regrettable that this practice generally stopped because these documents provide important links between the two parts of the Bible.[2] Without this material, the ordinary reader thinks a gulf, the so-called "400 silent years," exists between the Testaments. Historically there was no gulf, and the years were anything but silent.

The difference between the Jewish Bible and the Christian Bible is made by the presence of the New Testament, a collection of Christian literature written during the century prior to

[2] The Apocrypha is now available in the Revised Standard Version. It may be purchased separately or as part of the whole Christian Bible. A recent survey of its contents and a discussion of its role in Christianity is provided by Bruce Metzger, *An Introduction to the Apocrypha* (New York: Oxford University Press, 1957).

A.D. 150. (The phrases "The Old Testament" and "The New Testament" will be discussed later in this chapter.) Today, all Christians agree on the contents of the New Testament. It was not always so. It took several centuries before the precise limits of the New Testament were agreed upon. The oldest authoritative list of books which corresponds exactly with our Table of Contents comes from A.D. 367, three centuries after the earliest parts were written. Besides, the whole process was uneven. For example, it was several hundred years before all parts of the Church accepted the Epistle to the Hebrews, and other areas of Christendom did not accept the Letter of James or the Book of Revelation for over 400 years. Besides, almost from the start some churches used writings like the Letter of Barnabas or the so-called Shepherd of Hermas on virtually the same level as the letters of Paul. Later these books were excluded from the New Testament.[3]

[3] Early Christian literature not included in our New Testament has fallen into two categories. One is termed "The Apostolic Fathers" and includes the writings of important bishops like Clement of Rome (A.D. 95) and Ignatius of Antioch (A.D. 115), as well as anonymous documents like the Epistle of Barnabas, the Teaching of the Twelve Apostles, and the Shepherd of Hermas. A recent translation of this collection is offered by Edgar Goodspeed, *The Apostolic Fathers* (New York: Harper & Brothers, 1950). The rest are lumped together under the title "The New Testament Apocrypha." It includes early gospels (to which must be added the recently discovered Gospel of Thomas), acts, epistles, and revelations. This body of literature never enjoyed so important a role in the early Church as the Apostolic Fathers; none-

The point is that our Bible is a Scripture with a history. The communities of faith (the Synagogue and the Church) formed their Bibles by selecting certain documents and excluding others. Unfortunately, we can trace this Bible-making process in detail only for the New Testament and it is a far too complex process to be narrated here. But we can note the basic issues.

• The Church asked two important questions of each document: (1) Does it come from the first generations of Christians, particularly from the Apostles or their associates? (2) Does it contain what the Apostles taught? These questions were directed at two problems. The first question was aimed at the fact that after A.D. 100 the churches [4] were using all sorts of writings. For example, by A.D. 150 the twenty-seven books now in the New Testament would represent about half of the literature that was available to the church at Rome. Moreover, this growing body of literature represented a wide spectrum of convictions. Hence, when the Church became embroiled in controversies over belief and practice, it became necessary to have a list of authorities which everyone recognized. In making such a list,

---

theless, it shows the great variety of literature produced by the early Church. This diverse material is now available in the translation by M. R. James, *The Apocryphal New Testament* (New York: Oxford University Press, rev. ed., 1953).

[4] In this essay, the word "church" is capitalized when it refers to the entire Christian community. It remains uncapitalized when it refers primarily to a local congregation.

the first hurdle was apostolic authorship because most stripes of opinion respected the Apostles. The second was more subtle: Does the book contain what the Apostles taught? This question was important because more and more writings were circulating under the names of important Apostles—Peter, Paul, James, John, Thomas, and others. Since all writings circulating under the name of Paul, for example, did not agree, it was clear that some were forged in his name. Anyone who appealed to Paul for support had to know he was appealing to what was genuinely from Paul. By requiring a document to contain what the Apostles taught, therefore, the Church was not simply glorifying the Founding Fathers but exercising its responsibility to provide some sort of assurance that the Scripture contains authentic writings. By requiring that the New Testament books contain what the Apostles taught, the Church was not trying to freeze its development to the past, but was making sure that its ongoing life and thought be *in line* with the past. Determining what literature would become its New Testament by asking these two questions was a way of doing this, because this designated which writings from the earliest days would exert a pace-setting influence for the future.

But there is another side to the coin. The authority of this literature did not begin with the decision to admit it to the New Testament. Actually, the reverse is the more true—that the decision of the Church confirmed the authority which these documents already had and which

[30

the churches already had recognized by using them. In other words, the churches used this literature in worship, teaching, preaching and theological probing *before* the Church determined what would be Scripture. To a large extent, the life of the Church had already sifted the early Christian literature and found these to be the most incisive, the most effective, the most significant. The action of the Church in selecting twenty-seven books to be the New Testament reflected the power of the literature to be relevant from one generation to the next. The debates over what documents were to be excluded did not affect the heart of the New Testament at all, but were concerned primarily with the more peripheral writings like James, II Peter, Jude, or Revelation.

This means that the community of faith stands in a *two-sided relation to its Scripture*. On the *one* hand, the literature was written by the members of the Church in the first place, transmitted by the Church which used it in the second place, and declared to be Scripture by the Church in the third place. On the *other* hand, the literature was used and transmitted because it manifested its ability to contribute to the life of the Church in the first place, was declared to be Scripture in recognition of this in the second place, and continues to exercise its influence (sometimes even against the Church) in the third place. In short, the Church is not sovereign over the Bible as much Catholic thought suggests; nor does the Bible stand completely outside the Church as a heaven-sent answer-book as much Protestant thought implies. The Bible is an historical book produced within and for an historical community; at the same time, it enjoys its status as Scripture because men find themselves and their Church judged and summoned by it. Making this literature Scripture was the Church's way of saying something like the following: "Through this literature as through no other writings from our earlier brothers we continue to find ourselves addressed by God. Therefore, it shall be our Bible."

• However, modern scholarship does not always support the conviction of the early Church about the authorship of New Testament books. Scholars continue to debate the authorship of many books; their arguments need not detain us, but we should observe that there is such a discussion and note its consequences. The issue is this: What shall we do with a document if scholars conclude the Church erred in its judgment about the author?

We may open the question by observing that virtually all Protestant scholars deny that Paul wrote the so-called Epistle to the Hebrews. Roman Catholic scholars, on the other hand, continue to affirm that Paul was the author because the Biblical Commission took this position. The point is important because the Epistle to the Hebrews entered the New Testament precisely because the early Church came to believe Paul wrote it. Since the book became Scripture on this basis, should the conclusion that this was wrong lead Protestants to remove it from the New Testament? To the issue involved we say three things.

First, such a step is impossible for pragmatic reasons. There is no non-Catholic body with sufficient authority to add or subtract from the Bible. Any tampering with the list of New Testament books would be rejected by all sides. For precisely the same reason it is impossible to add a fifth gospel, even if an absolutely authentic one from Peter or James, for instance, should be discovered. The practical impossibility of modifying the content of the Bible clearly underscores the fact that the Church created the Bible by determining its contents. There is no body with sufficient authority for all Christendom today, not even for Protestantism, to change the Bible.

The second thing to be said can be illustrated better by referring to the Letter of Paul to Titus, his associate. Many scholars are convinced that Paul did not write this letter, at least in its present form. Even if scholars could agree that Paul did not write it (and if they could convince the Church at large), the appropriate step would not be to remove Titus from the Bible. Rather, because the Church applied two tests, authorship and content, the decisive question is not who wrote the book but what it says. To remove Titus from the New Testament, then, one would have to show that its contents were incompatible with the Christianity of Paul or the rest of the Apostles. There is no doubt that Titus has a somewhat different concept of Christianity from that found elsewhere in the New Testament, and even from certain of the unquestioned letters of Paul. But the question is not whether there are differences among the books but whether they are of such magnitude that they are incompatible with the New Testament as a whole. This is manifestly not the case, and so Titus remains, regardless of scholars' conclusions about the author.

There is still a third point to be noted. Even though Christians agree that the list of New Testament books should remain unchanged, each reader does, in fact, have his own preferences—his own Scripture within Scripture, so to speak. An examination of most well-used Bibles usually reveals sections with pages virtually as crisp as they were when the volume was bound. Many Christians find books like Obadiah and Zephaniah, Revelation, Jude, II Peter, II and III John unessential to their faith and life. Therefore such books actually stand outside their *functioning* Scripture even though they would not want to remove them from the Bible. For other people (and denominations as well) Daniel, Ezekiel, Revelation, II Peter, and Jude, are much more used than Isaiah, Romans, or Mark. This situation—that the parts of the Bible actually relied on vary from reader to reader—reflects the fact that *the Bible functions as Scripture as it is brought to bear on the actual faith and life of the readers.* The Bible's "Scripturehood" is established not simply by the Church's past decision about its contents but by each reader's ongoing use. This is the pragmatic test of what is actually our Scripture.

As the Church faced new problems, it continued to use the literature from its earliest members and eventually made a normative selection called the New Testament. It is one thing, however, for the Church to make the New Testament from its own literature. It is another matter when the Church appropriates someone else's Bible altogether. This is exactly what the Church did when it made the Synagogue's Bible into the Christian Old Testament. This is the next fact about our kind of Bible that we must explore.

Why Do We Keep the Jewish Bible?

The major part of the Christian Scripture is Jewish: 39 out of 66 books. Why should the Church accept the Bible of a faith which rejects what is central to Christianity—the conviction that Jesus is Christ, the Son of God? The Christian Bible does not appropriate a single sentence of the Hindu or Islamic Scripture; why should it accept the entire Jewish Bible?

• Actually, it is ironic that we should ask this question, because all the first Christians were Jews. Their only Bible was that of the Synagogue and they expected neither a replacement nor a supplement. Had anyone suggested that they abandon their Jewish Bibles because they believed in Jesus, they would have responded with appropriate vehemence.

But the earliest Christians kept the Synagogue Bible not simply because they were conservative Jews but because they were daring Christians.

35]

That is, they dared believe that Jesus was the Christ. We commonly use the phrase "Jesus Christ" as if it were a proper name like George Smith. Actually "Christ" is simply a transliteration of the Greek *Christos* (Latin: *Christus*) which translates a Hebrew word *Meshiach* (Messiah). Messiah is not a name at all but a title; it can be translated "anointed." Hence it is actually more correct to say "Jesus the Christ" or "Jesus who is called the Christ." If we want to understand why the earliest Christians kept the Hebrew Bible, we must know what they meant when they said Jesus was the Christ.

We may cut to the core of this rich idea by recalling that the Messiah was one of the figures expected to inaugurate the New Order at the end of history. The Jews expected that the Messiah would lead them in fulfilling their God-given destiny of bringing truth and justice to the nations, and of enjoying sovereignty and stability themselves. Since the people were now scattered abroad and oppressed by Romans at home, the Messiah was to be a victorious general in a holy war. The hope for the future took many forms and not all of them included a Messiah. But those which did understood him to be God's human agent empowered to free his people and rule them (and sometimes the world) in the name of God.

It was audacious for the first Christians to say Jesus was the Messiah. They asserted this primarily because they believed God raised him from the dead.[5] This belief brought three important consequences. (a) The conception of the Messiah had to be modified. Jesus clearly did not liberate his people nor did he achieve any political sovereignty. In fact, within a century the Romans crushed two revolts, destroyed Jerusalem twice, and ended political Messianism until its secularized form returned in modern Zionism. Hence, to call Jesus the Messiah was possible only if the idea were radically changed. This was

[5] The tradition of the first Christian preaching expresses this: "God has made him both Lord and Christ" [by resurrecting him]. This shows that the earliest believers held Jesus to have been installed in his Messianic role by the resurrection. As the term "Christ" became a proper name, the term "Lord" was used to express the belief in the sovereignty of the resurrected one. The Church naturally looked on his prior earthly life as the decisive preliminary phase of his total career.

Still, there is considerable doubt whether Jesus thought of himself as the Messiah. Clearly, he understood himself as playing the decisive role in the consummation of God's purpose; at the same time, however, he refused to detract from his mission by making his proper classification or title a primary matter for discussion. Believers are more concerned to classify Jesus than he was. For our purpose in this essay, it is important to note that even if Jesus had claimed to be the Messiah or the Son of Man or the Son of God, this would not have proved that he was. In fact, from the way his career ended most contemporaries concluded that he was an imposter. Moreover, by abandoning Jesus at the end, the disciples themselves gave mute eloquence to their disillusionment: Jesus had been wrong and those who engineered his death were basically right (see Luke 24:13-24). Only the resurrection, an act of God himself, made it clear and certain that Jesus was indeed God's man. This conviction came only to those to whom he appeared or to those who believed the announcement that God had raised him from the dead (see Luke 24:25-35).

done by pruning away the nationalist motif and emphasizing the transcendant and moral aspects of Jesus' Messiahship. The fact that already within twenty years of Jesus' death, Paul used "Christ" as if it were a proper name shows that the transformation was made very soon.

(b) At the same time, by insisting that Jesus was the Messiah (Christ) they asserted that Jesus fulfilled God's intent for Israel. Saying that the Messiah had arrived in Jesus meant that in him the purpose of Israel's existence had been achieved. Consequently, it could be maintained that when Gentiles believed in Jesus as Messiah, God's purpose for Israel had been attained, for in this way the Gentile converts were made participants in Israel's life. Thus, Israel's destiny of being a "light to the nations" was actually being fulfilled, not by the kind of Messiah that was expected but by this quite "unmessianic" Jesus.

(c) They found the clue to the meaning of Israel in the Bible, for here Israel's history was told and interpreted. This brought two developments. On the one hand, the Christians used their Bibles to show how Israel's true meaning was actualized in Jesus. In other words, they read the Synagogue Bible as a Christian book. On the other hand, the earliest Christians inferred that being a Christian meant being also a Jew. Hence at first all Gentile converts accepted the rites and customs of Judaism as well. Largely as the result of Paul's work and argument, this position was abandoned. Consequently, one could believe in Jesus without becoming a practicing Jew, for

[38

Paul argued that the Gentile became a "Jew" by virtue of his faith in Jesus. This provided inward participation in Israel's life; this was what mattered. At the same time, Paul insisted that the Gentile Christian must find the clue to his life in the Bible, for Jesus fulfilled its meaning. Consequently, neither Jewish nor Gentile Christians could repudiate the Bible of the Synagogue without rejecting this inner connection with Israel as well. Unfortunately, such a step was not long in coming.

• Within a century of Paul's time, there came a strong effort to rid the Church of the Jewish Bible altogether. The movement was led by Marcion from northern Asia Minor. Marcion considered himself a disciple of Paul and is the most important figure in the story of why the Christian Scripture has an Old Testament.

When Marcion read Paul's letters, especially the one sent to the Galatians in central Asia Minor, he noticed that Paul insisted that Gentile Christians need not become practicing Jews in order to be Christians. Paul said they were free from "the Law"—Paul's term for the forms, rites, and religion of Judaism. (By Marcion's time, however, Christianity had long been a primarily Gentile faith.) Marcion also noted that the reason Paul argued so vigorously was that Jewish Christians opposed him. Marcion then observed a third thing, that not only were the churches using the Jewish Bible but that Paul's letters sanctioned this by quoting it and arguing from it. Putting these three observations together, Marcion concluded that after Paul's death, the "Judaizers" had succeeded in reversing the message of Paul: they had related Christianity to Judaism much more closely than Paul did and had tampered with the letters of Paul to make it appear that he had advocated this.

Once he had seen the situation in these terms, Marcion's task was clear: he would be the first Reformer! He would restore Christianity to its (supposed) Pauline form. He set about editing the letters of Paul by removing the objectionable paragraphs. He went even farther; rejecting all Gospels as too Jewish except Luke, he edited this Gospel because he insisted that the distorters had made even Jesus appeal to the Jewish Bible. Thus Marcion offered the Church the first clear-cut Christian Bible in the form of an abbreviated edition of Luke and the letters of Paul. Marcion did not view this as a "New Testament" to be placed beside the Synagogue Bible; rather, Marcion intended to replace the old Bible altogether. *Marcion offered the Church a completely new Bible.*

Marcion's movement had alarming appeal. After moving westward through Asia Minor, he arrived in Rome where he tried to reform that church. It was in no mood to be reformed and it excommunicated him in July, A.D. 144. Marcion immediately formed his own Church and was eminently successful. The traditional Church considered the Marcionites a major threat for decades; they were not stamped out until two centuries later, when the Church had the power of the Byzantine state behind it.

Actually, there were many more issues involved than the role of the Jewish Bible. Marcion's fundamental problem was his dualistic outlook on the world. To him, man's root problem was his existence in evil matter ruled by a heartless law of tooth and fang. Marcion was just as impressed with the inexorability of nature and its laws as we are, even though he had far less scientific data to buttress his convictions. What made Marcion so firmly opposed to Judaism and its Bible was the fact that man's abysmal situation is the work of the Creator, the God described in Genesis and worshiped by the Jews. The only conceivable relation Christianity could have with this situation was rescue and rejection. Thus Marcion insisted that Jesus was sent by another God, a good God, to rescue men from the Creator so that they might reject his influence. Marcion insisted that Jesus came from a God who was completely unknown prior to the arrival of Jesus in Galilee; this is why the Jewish Bible knows nothing about him or the God who sent him. It does, however, provide ample documentation for the character of the Creator. Marcion delighted in finding passages which emphasized the Creator's justice, wrath, or vengeance. These he contrasted with statements about God's love and mercy drawn from the words of Jesus or Paul. Sentences like Isaiah 45:7 were especially useful: "I [God the Creator] form light and create darkness; I make weal and create woe." And to

41]

show that Jesus came to reveal an entirely different kind of God he could quote Luke 10:22: "All things have been delivered to me by my Father; and no one knows who the Son is except the Father or who the Father is except the Son and any one to whom the Son chooses to reveal him."

It is clear that Marcion not only provided a completely new Bible but offered a way of reading the old one so as to make it speak in his favor. Marcion rejected the idea that the Synagogue Bible could be read as a Christian book. What was at stake was the conception of man, the character of God, the work of Jesus, and the history of the Church.

• The Church's response was immediate and thorough. Besides expelling Marcion, it took three positive steps to counter his influence. (a) It rose to debate the theological issues. Consequently the creeds affirm that Christians believe in "God the Father Almighty, maker of heaven and earth" and not in some unknown deity who waited in obscurity before deciding to rescue men from creation. (b) It created its own collection of Christian literature consisting not of only one Gospel but of four; this collection also contained the letters not of one apostle only but of five (Paul, Peter, James, John, and Jude). Between these two parts of the collection it inserted the Book of the Acts of the Apostles, and after the second part it appended the Book of Revelation. As we have noted before, the entire process took more than two centuries before complete agree-

[42

ment was reached, but the intent was clear from the start: the Church looked to all the apostles. (c) The Church also insisted that the Bible of the Synagogue be retained in its Bible, as it had been from the start. The new collection was simply placed beside it. Now the phrase "The Bible" meant two collections, known as the Old and New Testaments. From this position there has been no retreat.

Despite the fact that the Church settled the matter in Marcion's time, we now feel compelled to open the question again and ask whether our Bible does have any genuine unity. That is, does it have a basically unified message, or is it simply held together by the decree of the Church? Today one can buy the parts of the Bible separately. Is this perhaps the most appropriate way for it to circulate?

Is It Really One Bible?

The Church kept the old Bible in its Scripture not simply because it believed Jesus was the Messiah but also because it believed it was the true Israel. In the Church, people from all sorts of religious and racial backgrounds were united by faith in Jesus and by using the Jewish Bible; here they found the clue to the meaning of his life and theirs. These Christians found the term "testament" an appropriate way to think of their relation to Israel and to Israel's God.

• We know the term "testament" from its use in legal matters, especially in the phrase "last will and testament." Actually, this helps us to under-

43]

stand its biblical meaning. To get the real brunt of the matter, we must begin with the Hebrew equivalent, *berith,* which means compact, treaty, covenant. We are familiar with this term also, since it is used in Jewish circles as B'nai B'rith— sons of the covenant. The Hebrew Bible used the word for agreements between persons or nations; it is a negotiable contract binding both parties. The same term is used for the relation of God and man, especially God and Israel. The Hebrew Bible dares to use this legal and commercial term because it has no doubt that the initiative lies with God. We may put this into legal jargon: when used for the relation between God and Israel, *berith is a unilaterally initiated agreement with bilateral responsibility.*[6]

When the Hebrew Bible was translated into Greek, the translators used the word *diatheke*

[6] Genesis 15 tells how God and Abraham made a *berith.* The story reports no negotiation; God appears to make his promise and elicit Abraham's response. The compact is consummated by cutting animals in halves which then are placed opposite each other, a ritual representing the bilateral character of the agreement. The flaming torch that passes between the halves symbolizes the divine Presence. This story, so embedded in ancient Semitic ideas, accents God's role as the initiator, stipulator, and guarantor of the agreement. Abraham's role is limited to accepting the terms. In Genesis 17, the later editors of the tradition have told the story again, this time making explicit what was implied in Chapter 15: God announces that he will establish this covenant, set its terms, and see to its fulfillment. In the story of Israel's escape from Egypt (Exodus 1-15) the covenant theme is even stronger. This event, coupled with the experience at Mount Sinai (Exodus 19ff.) became the most important element in Israel's understanding of herself and God.

because this term was used when people settled the disposition of property, just as we use the term "testament" today. Thus the translators caught the true import of the Hebrew Bible's insistence that the people of Israel are related to God by a compact whose terms God alone had set. The whole idea of Israel as the chosen people of God is expressed in the term *berith*, covenant, testament. This term provided a fundamental way of saying that God had committed himself to this people, and thereby had committed them to himself and his purpose. Whether we find the covenant congenial or not, the fact is that neither the Old Testament nor the history of the Jews is intelligible without it.

The earliest Christians, being Jews, stood within this point of view. So did the Gentiles who were converted to Christianity. Two elements fostered this outlook. One was the promise of the prophet Jeremiah (sixth century B.C.) who peered beyond the destruction of his country to the day when God would grant a new covenant with his people, one which included not simply moral conduct but inward transformation as well (Jeremiah 31:34). The other was Christian worship which centered in the Lord's Supper; here believers remembered the words of Jesus, that in his death God offered men a new covenant, a new relationship (Mark 14:22-25, I Corinthians 11:23-26). To the Christian community, the expectation of Jeremiah was now fulfilled in Christianity. Thus, if what is expected in the Jewish Bible is achieved in Christianity, then the Church

45]

is the object of this hope. Moreover, whereas Judaism spoke of its covenant with God as established through Abraham and Moses, the Church spoke of its covenant made in the life-death-resurrection of Jesus.

• After this mode of understanding Jesus and the Church took root it was a short step to label the Jewish Bible as the Books of the Old Covenant; nor was it long before the Christian literature was called the Books of the New Covenant, or simply the New Testament.

To the Christian community, then, the Bible is composed of two testaments dealing with God's commitments, first to Israel and then to the Church. It is of fundamental importance to remember that basically these testaments are not documents at all, as though they were analogous to the charter of the League of Nations and that of the United Nations. Originally, neither covenant was a document but a historical event. In the case of Israel, it was the migration of Abraham and the liberation of Israel; in the case of the Church, it was the life-death-resurrection of Jesus. In each case, the events are understood as occurrences in which God and the community are committed to one another.

The real unity of our Christian Bible, then, lies in the covenants between God and the community of faith, the Church. Apart from the conviction that Jesus is the focal point (the fulfillment of God's purpose for Israel), no real unity can be seen. All that can be established is the historical continuity given by the fact that the first

[46

Christians were Jews. Had Marcion been successful in claiming that Jesus was not the fulfillment of Judaism but the means for man's escape from it, no unity would have been possible. We Gentiles who affirm that Jesus is the Christ implicitly admit that in a profound sense we share in two covenants and are members of two communities: the Church and its predecessor, Israel. In this sense, believing in Jesus makes us all sons of Abraham. This is why we have one Bible in two Testaments.

WHEN SCHOLARS
GO TO WORK

3

SATURDAY'S CHURCH ADS in a metropolitan newspaper reveal a religious jungle. Most of this bewildering assortment of denominations, cults, and societies claim to offer the real meaning of life and the true meaning of the Bible. In fact, the whole history of the Church is largely a history of trying to come to terms with the Bible. Similarly, each denomination has claimed to represent the Bible most adequately. Those who teach in interdenominational theological schools are often asked how they get away with it—a Baptist, for instance, teaching Methodist, Disciple, Presbyterian, and Church of Christ students what the Bible means. People ask for an explanation because they do not realize that today there is a commitment to the scholarly understanding of the Bible which runs deeper than a commitment to a purely denominational understanding. When seen in the light of twenty centuries of Christianity, this is a new develop-

49]

ment. It is possible because there is widespread agreement that the Bible must not be exempt from the rules of the scholar's game.

Who Has the Last Word?

• The Protestant reformers were biblical scholars. Although the theoretical issues concerned man's relation to God, the reformers insisted this had to be settled by the "plain sense of Scripture." They believed they were not irresponsible innovators but interpreters of what the Bible actually said and intended to say. This conviction turned out to be decisive, for it implied that the meaning of Scripture was not determined by what the theologians decreed but by what the words of the text actually meant. The reformers insisted that Scripture, read in this way, was the ultimate authority. The Catholic instinct correctly realized the radical character of the Protestant proposal, for the reformers claimed the Church had misunderstood its own Bible. Moreover, they held that the life and thought of the Church must be corrected by what the Bible intended to say. Although the reformers did not actually say so, this meant that in effect, the grammarians, lexicographers, and historians could reform the Church because they knew better than the bishops what the Bible actually meant. The Reformation demanded that the Church reform its sacred theology on the basis of profane study; that is, by what competent scholars concluded

[50

the text intended to say. The Reformation was largely a scholars' reform.[1]

So revolutionary was this proposal that Protestantism has hardly been able to live with it. After Protestantism jelled into its own orthodoxy and traditionalism, it was seldom flexible enough to ·correct itself by the scholar's conclusions. Like the earlier Church which it tried to reform, Protestantism assumed it knew in advance what the Bible meant. The scholar's task, in such case, was to provide learned documentation but no correction.

This outlook is still alive. It can be seen in the arguments that raged over the way Isaiah 7:14 was translated in the Revised Standard Version. The King James Version of 1611 reads: "Behold, a virgin shall conceive. . . ." Ever since the Gospel according to Matthew quoted this as evidence that Jesus fulfilled the Old Testament even in his birth (Matthew 1:23), Christians have assumed that Isaiah predicted the Virgin Birth. But the matter is not so simple. For one thing, Matthew quotes the Greek Bible, the Septuagint. The

[1] The point is well made by E. H. Harbison, *The Christian Scholar in the Age of the Reformation* (New York: Charles Scribner's Sons, 1956), p. vi. He writes, "The Protestant Reformation began in a scholar's insight into the meaning of Scripture. It was to a large extent a learned movement, a thing of professors and students, a scholar's revolution. . . . The Catholic response . . . partook of the same nature. The prestige and influence of Christian scholars probably never stood higher in all of Western history than during the two generations which embraced the lifetimes of Erasmus, Luther, and Calvin."

trouble is that scholars conclude this verse is not accurately translated. The Hebrew word means simply "maiden" or "young girl"; her virginity may be assumed but it is not pointed out. Scholars correctly translated the verse according to its normal Hebrew meaning and not according to the Greek translation or Matthew's quotation. Consequently, this translation suggests that Isaiah did not predict the Virgin Birth. Now the issue is clear: who knows what Isaiah meant— Matthew (and the Church) or modern students of ancient Hebrew? Must the Church modify its understanding of Isaiah because a group of scholars reach this conclusion? The Protestant principle answers "Yes." This is why many non-Catholics find it so hard to be real Protestants.

This controversy illustrates how important scholarship has become for understanding the Bible. The decisive factor in the translators' decision was a historical judgment and not a theological conviction. In other words, the crucial point was what the author intended to say. Therefore, the fundamental emphasis in biblical study is not simply "what it means to me now" but what the writer meant to say then. The only reliable way of learning this is by using the accepted methods of historical study. That is, we learn what the Apostle Paul, for example, wanted to say in his letters by precisely the same method we learn what Calvin or Cicero wanted to say in theirs. Reading the Bible this way does not rule out inspirational reading, but it does insist that we know what the writers wanted to say only by historical study. There are no short cuts.

• Unfortunately, some people continue to resist this outlook. They see the need for using historical criticism for certain matters of biblical study like language or history. But they are unwilling to let the historian have the decisive word about what the Bible means. Since for them the Bible is God's own Word, these Christians insist that we develop a special, sacred method for this special, sacred literature. Beginning with the assertion that the Bible is God's inspired and therefore perfect Book, they demand that this conviction control all study of it, even the conclusions which the historian is permitted to draw.[2]

Though there are many reasons why such a stance is unsatisfactory, we select two. (a) The

[2] An example of this is the work of L. Berkhof, *Principles of Biblical Interpretation* (Grand Rapids, Mich.: Baker Book House, 1950). This highly conservative Calvinist argues that because biblical interpretation "deals with a book that is unique in the realm of literature, *viz.*, with the Bible as the inspired Word of God," we must develop a sacred interpretative science of a "very special character (page 11). Consequently, he does not hesitate to say that when one finds solid historical evidence which conflicts "not with his interpretation of the Bible, but . . . with the Bible itself . . . there is only one legitimate course, *viz.*, to cling faithfully to the statement of the Bible, and to wait patiently for additional light" (131f.). In the same vein, right-wing conservatives insist that Moses actually wrote the entire Pentateuch (first five Books of the Bible) despite the overwhelming literary and linguistic evidence to the contrary; they do so primarily because the Bible can be quoted to the effect that Moses wrote it. See for example Merrill F. Unger, *Introductory Guide to the Old Testament* (Grand Rapids, Mich.: Zondervan Publishing House, 1951, Chs. II, VIII).

Bible does not need to be protected from historical study. The zealot thinks he must guard the Bible lest the historian and the literary critic destroy
it. He does not realize that he may be so intent to
preserve the Book and a doctrine about it that he
misses the point of the Book itself. One should
not be afraid to ask the Bible directly what it has
to say. Even the person who believes strongly that
the Bible is God's own Word should be willing to
let it speak for itself, on its own terms and in its
own way. This is precisely what the historian aims
to do—penetrate the literature so that, as far as
possible, the writer may communicate with his
modern reader as he once did with his contemporaries. This takes diligent use of all the tools of
historical study.

(b) The Bible itself requires historical study
because it is pre-eminently concerned with history. Judaism and Christianity not only tolerate
historical analysis of their Bibles but insist that
this be a fundamental part of the training of their
clergy. This is unique in the history of religion.
Both faiths emphasize historical criticism because
they focus on the religious meanings of historical
events. They realize that events can have no
meaning if they are not understood; conversely,
the more one knows about the events the sharper
faith's meanings may be. Thus, the character of
the Bible itself and the communities for whom it
is Scripture ask for historical study. Both faiths
use historical study to keep from inflating themselves with religious fantasy or speculation. In
addition, historical study keeps attention focused

on important questions about our own history, including that of the individual reader.

The rest of this chapter will show briefly how historical study of the Bible proceeds and the kinds of questions it leads the Bible and its readers to ask one another. In this way we hope to show how such work affects the way we understand what the Bible says and what it is.

What Are Scholars Doing to the Bible?

Scholars distinguish among three kinds of work: literary criticism, historical reconstruction, and theological analysis. These should never be carried on in isolation from each other; they should, however, be distinguished for the sake of clean method.

• Literary criticism is the foundation of all biblical study and was the first to be developed in the modern period. Two phases have been distinguished. One aims to find out what the writer actually wrote; the other attempts to understand what he wrote in the light of his circumstances.

The basic question is, What did the author actually write? Even after centuries of work, there is no complete agreement on this issue. The reason is that we do not have an original manuscript of a single book in the Bible (technically called the Autograph). Therefore the text critic tries to determine what was originally written. He has three basic sources: hand copies of hand copies of the original (the manuscripts in Hebrew or Greek), early translations into ancient languages like Latin or Syriac, and the quotations

55]

of the Bible found in early Christian literature.
With painstaking skill and attention to detail, he
tries to determine what Luke, for example, actually wrote. In spite of the thousands of Greek
manuscripts, an abundance of quotations and a
handful of ancient translations, there is an amazing amount of agreement so that in most cases
we are more confident of the text of the New
Testament than of any other literature of the
period. Yet, there are many instances in which
we simply are not sure what the author wrote.
Hence every English Bible is not only the trans-
lator's understanding of what the text means but
also the text critic's judgment of what it actually
says. Fortunately, the new translations print important alternatives in the footnotes. But even
where no alternate phrases are printed, the wording of the Bible is the result of a critical judgment
of all the evidence.

It is amazing how fundamentalism [3] talks so

[3] In this essay, the term "fundamentalism" is used
loosely to characterize right-wing Protestantism in general. The term has a checkered history. After a confer-
ence at Niagara Falls in 1895 said that five doctrines
were of fundamental importance, twelve volumes of essays, called *Fundamentals,* were published privately and
circulated free in 1909. The five doctrines are (1) divine
inspiration of every word of the original copies of the
Bible (verbal inspiration) resulting in complete absence
of all error (infallibility); (2) the literal, biological fact
of Jesus' Virgin Birth (as opposed to symbolic or poetic
interpretations); (3) the literal atoning work of Jesus'
blood; (4) physical resurrection; (5) bodily return of
Jesus from heaven (Second Coming). The term "fundamentalist" naturally became the label for militant advocates of these points. Probably, "literalist" would be

confidently about the inerrant, perfect, infallible character of the original Autographs of the Bible when no one has seen one for more than eighteen centuries! Moreover, it is clear that originally no one thought the wording was perfect since copyists, translators, and authors had little fear of changing it. This is one reason the text critic's task is so complex. He aims to unravel these changes in order to provide a text which is reasonably reliable. He has no perfect text to offer.

The other kind of literary criticism, misnamed "Higher Criticism," studies the circumstances in which the original text was written. Since most of the Bible is anonymous, we want to know who the actual authors were; moreover, we want to

---

more accurate. In a way, fundamentalism is as much a frame of mind as a set of doctrines, for many Christians hold these convictions without repudiating those who differ.

In recent years, fundamentalism has become more sophisticated, and many are fleeing the term whenever possible, preferring the term Evangelical or Orthodox. The major voice of sophisticated fundamentalism is the journal *Christianity Today*, a recent imitator of the *Christian Century*. Fundamentalist churches have formed the National Association of Evangelicals, a counterpart to the National Council of Churches; they have also organized the International Council of Christian Churches as a parallel to the World Council of Churches. On college campuses, sophisticated fundamentalism is represented by the Inter-Varsity Fellowship and it provides its own journal as well, *The Collegiate Challenge*. An example of a completely unsophisticated, old-line fundamentalist journal is *The Sword of the Lord*, which looks on many conservatives as being "soft on liberalism." Recently, conversation has been resumed between sophisticated fundamentalists and the other wings of Protestantism; this is clearly a good omen.

know if the names now associated with documents, like Moses or Mark, are reliable. We also want to know whether the document was written as it now stands or whether it has been compiled and edited. We are interested also in the time and place of writing, the original readers, and the issues that evoked the literature in the first place. These questions are standard inquiries in all literary criticism. Yet it is around such questions that furious battles have raged in the Church. Consequently, we note first why this kind of work caused such controversy; then we note how the historian relates the biblical literature to its original setting.

The Book of Isaiah illustrates the issue and the conflict. This Old Testament document has 66 chapters introduced as "The Vision of Isaiah." We want to know whether Isaiah of Jerusalem (eighth century B.C.) wrote the entire Book or whether the different styles, vocabulary, and concerns indicate additions to it. Chapters 1-39 are addressed to eighth-century Jews living in Jerusalem; Chapters 40-66 assume the Jews are exiled in Mesopotamia two hundred years later. When a critic finds such a situation in other literature, he concludes that the last section was written two centuries later and was simply added to the earlier work. Biblical scholars reach the same conclusion about Isaiah.

But fundamentalists have objected strenuously. Without denying the data on which the conclusion was based, they insist that it has been over-emphasized and wrongly understood. Because fundamentalists believe the Bible was divinely inspired in such a way as to exclude any error, they hold it is impossible to detach Chapters 40-66 from a book which claims to be from Isaiah. Moreover, they insist that the situation presupposed in these chapters was divinely revealed two centuries before. Consequently, they argue, what is at stake is whether or not such a prediction was made to Isaiah. For this reason those who insist that the book is compiled are accused of "denying the Bible." The fundamentalists have correctly seen that if one concludes Chapters 40-66 were written during the later situation (and not a prediction of it) they must change their conception of the Bible, and perhaps their understanding of God as well.

The basic principle is that we must separate the theological issues (holding the Bible to be inspired Scripture) from literary questions. The problem of who wrote a passage is a strictly literary and historical problem. The question of how many men wrote the Book of Isaiah cannot be answered by quoting doctrines about the Bible but only by detailed study of the text. Every adequate conception of the Bible is willing to do this; it should also accept the consequences. The fundamentalist cannot really listen to the historian; nor can the Roman Catholic who must believe that Matthew's Gospel is older than Mark's, even though most critics insist that Matthew used Mark. Both the Catholics and the fundamentalists are willing to follow the critic so long as his con-

clusions bolster the answers they already have;
neither can afford to be corrected.

Such a position should be surrendered. The
historian must be free to reach whatever conclusion he believes the evidence requires, even if this
does not harmonize with tradition or doctrine.
Questions about the unity and authorship of a
book cannot be settled in terms of a scholar's
orthodoxy but solely on the basis of his com-
petence in assessing the evidence. This is the
Protestant principle, and when it is taken seriously one risks putting his conception of the Bible
into the hands of the scholar. It also means re-
thinking the authority of the kind of Bible which
scholarship shows it to be. This is what this book
attempts to do.

Having seen the kinds of issues raised by so-
called "Higher Criticism," we can now show how
this method actually functions and the questions
it forges for faith.

When we relate the Bible to its proper setting
in history, we first ask, "What happened to the
original manuscripts the authors wrote?" The text
critic cannot close the gap between our printed
text and the original because we know very little
about the transmission of the original copies. For
example, we have the letters of Paul only in collections made by the Church, and there is no
reason to think that the collection is complete.
Moreover, the Church edited what it collected.
Thus Romans 16 may have been added to the
rest of the book, and II Corinthians appears to
be made up of parts of at least three letters. The

same sort of thing can be said about other books, including those of the Old Testament. This reminds us that the Bible is the community's book. We have this literature because groups of people used, copied, and collected it. The hand of the community can be detected at every stage in the Bible's growth. This can never be forgotten.

The next step is to study the situation of the writer. Some parts of the Bible are completely unintelligible until the author is seen in his setting. For instance, the books of the prophets must be studied with one eye on the history of the ancient Near East because these men spoke to the problems posed by international affairs. The setting is important not only for understanding men like the prophet Amos or the Apostle Paul who speak directly to particular problems they face, but it is also vitally important for authors who write about historical events. This is because the situation of the writer shapes what he says about history and how he says it. A book review illustrates this very well; for the reviewer not only tells his reader about the book but, by the way he talks about it, he reveals himself as well.

A biblical example of this can be found in the stories of Jesus in the temple at Jerusalem. In Mark's Gospel, Jesus expelled the merchants the day after he rode into Jerusalem just before his death. Mark also reports (11:11-19) that Jesus said the temple was to be a house of prayer for all nations. Matthew and Luke follow Mark generally, but here they tell the story as the climax of the entry, thus putting the temple-scene a day earlier. Moreover, both omit the reference to the temple as the house of prayer for all nations (Matthew 21:1-17; Luke 19:45 f.). They omit this because in their day the temple was already destroyed by the Roman army; consequently, that temple clearly was not destined to be the house of prayer for all nations. John's Gospel (2:13-22) puts the event at the beginning of Jesus' ministry instead of near the end, because for John it symbolized Jesus' work in purifying Judaism. Our point is that each writer tells the incident in the light of his own situation.

With regard to Jesus, we could find many similar illustrations because we have four Gospels, each with its own setting in which it views and interprets Jesus. Parts of the Old Testament also are parallel accounts of the same period, such as the books of Joshua and Judges, Kings and Chronicles. But, whether we can trace it or not, we must recognize that both what is told and how it is reported are influenced by the situation. Since these differed as the life of the community went on, the presentation of history changed as well, whether it was the reign of David or the ministry of Jesus. This is such a fundamental matter that we shall return to it in Chapter Five.

The third step the historian takes is to seek the writer's sources. The traditional view is that the authors of the Bible needed no sources because God simply inspired them, that is, revealed what they should write. There is no way this can be demonstrated. But, even if one accepts this view, it does not follow that the writer was ignorant before he was inspired, or that inspiration made using ordinary sources unnecessary. In fact, the writer's inspiration probably consisted of insight into the traditions and resources available to him.

Luke's Gospel offers a clear example of a biblical writer's use of sources. Luke is one of the few writers who openly admits he used earlier writings (Luke 1:1-4), though the others clearly used them too. Luke used the Gospel of Mark to provide the basic outline. Because Luke was not satisfied with Mark, he supplemented it with other materials and modified the structure here and there. Besides, some additional material came from a collection (or series) of Jesus' teachings. Matthew used this also, and by comparing Matthew and Luke, scholars reconstruct this lost document. In addition, Luke used stories otherwise unknown to us, such as the story of the births of Jesus and John the Baptist or the parable of the prodigal son. Luke brought all this material together to write a fresh, vivid story of Jesus. By analyzing the ways Luke used his sources, it is possible to gauge his interests and emphases.

As a matter of fact, a careful study of the sources themselves shows that long before Luke found them, they had been shaped by the Christians who used them. For example, Luke 10:38-42 reports Jesus' visit with two sisters, Mary and Martha. The story omits the name of the village and all details of the situation except what is important—that Jesus chided the domestic Martha because she wanted Mary to stop listening to Jesus and help set the table. Moreover, only the heart of Jesus' comments is reported: "Martha, Martha, you are anxious and troubled about many things; one thing is needful. Mary has chosen the good portion, which shall not be taken away from her." Here the story breaks off, for it is interested only in this pronouncement and not in the reaction of Martha or the disciples. The Christians who told it had filtered out all details they did not think germane.[4]

The foregoing paragraphs rest on judgments about the Gospels which cannot be detailed here. They may not be universally accepted by scholars either. In such matters the layman has no choice but to inform himself as best he can (all sorts of tools are now readily available) and to accept

[4] In this century, scholars have analyzed biblical literature to see what traces remain from the time when the stories and sayings were *told* before they were written. This is a highly specialized research problem, and many of its "results" remain hypothetical. However, they shed important light on the way the community treated the traditions it used. This kind of study is termed Form Criticism because it began by studying the structure of the stories and sayings and proceeded to infer their functions in the community. After this method was worked out for the stories in the Book of Genesis, it was applied to the stories of Jesus in the Gospels. Much that we have said about the impact of the community's use on the stories themselves is rooted in a form-criticism approach to the tradition. Rudolf Bultmann, a leading New Testament form critic, has interpreted his work in "The New Approach to the Synoptic Problem" now included in his essays edited by Schubert Ogden, *Existence and Faith*— Meridian Living Age Books No. 29 (New York: Meridian Books, 1960).

the most convincing position. The matter is quite analogous to the problem of selecting components for a "hi fi" set; here too one finds less than unanimous judgments. Indeed, the music one will hear at home is in a real way affected by the decisions made in the store.

Furthermore, the writer's sources include not only documents but words and ideas. Therefore, interpreting the Bible in its historical setting also requires us to relate its ideas to the religious environment of the day. This aspect of study has frequently been misunderstood because some of its advocates prematurely concluded that the biblical writers simply borrowed their ideas from their surroundings. Such oversimplifications suggested that the Bible was not at all a revelation of God to men but a patchwork of ancient religious ideas. The recent excitement over the meaning of the Dead Sea Scrolls illustrates this perfectly. When certain writers found it was possible that early Christianity was influenced by the group that produced this material, they immediately concluded this jeopardized Christianity because it meant that it was nothing but old ideas warmed over in the name of Jesus. Such conclusions are perfectly silly. Biblical scholars and theologians are not at all disturbed at the possibility that certain Christian ideas might be found in the earlier Dead Sea Scrolls, or even stem from there, because they see that there is no need to insist on the absolute uniqueness of the Bible and that nothing is lost by seeing it in its true historical setting, whatever that might prove to be. Since

65]

the Bible is an historical book written in historical circumstances, then its ideas inevitably have certain parallels in the environment. The alternative to this would be a Bible written in a vacuum, and consequently useless. But it is of fundamental importance not only to see the similarities between certain biblical ideas and those found in its environment, but also to note the differences. The uniqueness of the Bible frequently lies in the *way* ideas, partly shared with the environment, are related to the mainstream of its faith. In short, the Bible emerged in a community of faith which had a definite cultural context. Reading such a Bible historically requires that we take both elements seriously.

We may conclude this sketch of literary criticism by pointing out that we constantly find an interaction between the community and the materials it transmits. We see it in the way the written documents were collected and edited for use in synagogues and churches; we note it in the way the authors adapted the materials they used in order to say something to their readers; we see how the earliest sources reflect the influence of the community and its context. Thus at every point in its development the Bible stands in a double relation to its context: it comes from the community (in a particular setting), but it reshapes its traditions so as to address it. The life of the community and the development of the Bible belong together.

• Once we understand the Bible as literature deeply rooted in the communities of faith, then we may take the next step—historical reconstruction. To be sure, the scholar does this all along. But now we point out that since the Bible talks about historical events, the scholar wants to study the events themselves and not simply the sources of information about them.

When the historian reconstructs the history of an event reported in the Bible, like the reign of David or the career of Paul, he brings together as many sources of information as possible: biblical accounts, archeological data, nonbiblical reports. Each of these, in turn, is understood in the light of its setting. But when the historian correlates all the data, the biblical stories carry no more weight than other materials. That is to say, the historian treats all sources of information in the same way. His conclusion about their reliability stems from his professional judgment as a historian. On the whole it can be said that the biblical reports have been verified by archeological materials.

But we must not fool ourselves by thinking that because the archeologist proved that Solomon did have a copper smelter on the Gulf of Aqaba and a horse-trading business at Megiddo, he has thereby demonstrated that the biblical understanding of Solomon is true. Archeological evidence deals with the context of the biblical story but not with its meanings for the Bible. Some writers have not always seen this clearly. Hence they imply that because new evidence confirms the cultural milieu of the Hebrew patriarch Abraham (*circa* 2000-1700 B.C.), it proves that the biblical account is correct. Actually, all the material does is to make it quite unlikely that the stories of Abraham were invented long afterward when the cultural details would have been forgotten. But mapping trails in the Negev and studying marital customs of the second millennium B.C. will not confirm what the Bible really wants to say about Abraham—that God made a covenant with him. In other words, *archeology does not prove the Bible. It only proves the Bible is concerned with real history,* but this is decisive.

There are, however, instances in which the historian's reconstruction does not verify the biblical account. Such a case is the Israelite conquest of Palestine. The Bible reports that Moses led the twelve tribes out of Egypt and that after forty years of desert migration they finally crossed the Jordan River from the east, captured nearby Jericho and proceeded to conquer the whole area by a series of eminently successful campaigns. The historian who analyzes the invasion produces a different picture, partly because he relies on scattered details in the rest of the Bible and partly because he correlates archeological material. He concludes that probably not all twelve tribes had been in Egypt nor had migrated together. Moreover, Jericho seems to have been destroyed long before. As in all historical study, we deal with probabilities. But even so, our point is that the historian's portrait of history must be taken seriously. The consequences of doing this will concern us again in Chapter Five. Here, we are concerned only to show the kinds of results historical study of the Bible sometimes has.

• Theological matters lie near the heart of this essay—the character of the Bible and what it has to say. We have dealt with literary and historical matters first because it is necessary to show what kind of Bible we are talking about. We have emphasized the complex development of our Bible. The fundamental theological matter before us now is whether such a Bible has any real unity. In the previous chapters we saw the kind of unity the early Church found. Our question now is whether *we* find any. Is the Bible basically a collection of individual interpretations of God's will, or do they together constitute a basic, unified message? Scholars have separated it into various strata and traditions; is there enough unity here to permit one to speak of "the biblical faith"? This essay contends that there is both continuity and unity in the Bible.

To begin, we see a continuity which results from the fact that the Bible was produced in a continuing community. But the continuity is deeper than this. The Old Testament grew out of Israelite faith responding to its environment. The fundamental axiom of this faith was the covenant with God, especially clarified in the exodus from Egypt and the experience at Mt. Sinai. Passover celebrates this annually. Some scholars think that the form of the story in Exodus 15 results from telling and retelling it during the festival. Someone simply wrote it down the way it came to be told. Wherever the festival was celebrated, the people would be reminded of the foundations of their faith: Israel was chosen by God, redeemed

by him from Egyptian bondage, was made a cov-
enant-partner with him at Sinai, continues to live
under the leadership of God who is concerned
for this covenant. Passover, together with other
festivals, provided a continuing matrix in which
the writers of the Bible stand. Besides, the Israelite hymnal (the Book of Psalms) contains many
hymns which celebrate the Israelite understanding of her history as the work of God (for example, Psalms 44, 68, 78, 80, 105, 114, 136). Israel's faith was sung as well as told.

Because the festivals and worship provided a
continuum of faith, the prophets could appeal to
the people to make their lives consistent with this
way of thinking about Israel. They can make such
an appeal because they have drunk deeply at the
well of this tradition; they also assume it is intelligible and fundamental to their hearers. We see
this in passages like Amos 3:1f., Hosea 11:1-9,
Jeremiah 31:31-34, Isaiah 51:1-16. The prophets
are critical because they see their contemporaries
ignoring the fundamental meanings of this history which is celebrated in festival and worship.

In the New Testament, the case is perfectly
analogous. This time the fundamental point of
departure is the life-death-resurrection of Jesus
understood as God's decisive act. Instead of the
Passover, it is the Lord's Supper which reminds
the believers of their faith. This is the common
ground on which the writers and the readers
stand. Moreover, the Lord's Supper and the death
of Jesus occurred during the Passover festival,

thus providing a strong link between the two communities.

The historical method, then, does not simply locate the varieties of materials and traditions in the Bible, but it also helps us to detect the pulse which surges through the whole Bible. This unifying pulse is the worship of the ongoing community. This worship links each generation to those before and after it.

Consequently, the unity of the Bible is not found in a comprehensive system of doctrine of theology. Rather, it is its persistent preoccupation with history understood as the medium by which God meets man. The unity is found not in a set of concepts but in a mode of understanding history. This way of looking at history is celebrated and nurtured by the community at worship, because here the community seeks the presence of the God who has disclosed himself in the community's history. What holds the Bible together is not a pervasive system but a persistent stance.

This is why the Bible is so little concerned with orthodoxy (except certain later parts of the New Testament). The Bible is not so interested in teaching a doctrine about God as it is in eliciting a kind of relationship to him. The Israelites did not celebrate Passover simply to preserve their memories or to teach ideas about the exodus, but to remind each person that because he was an Israelite, he participated in that event and therefore was a responsible partner to the covenant. Similarly, the New Testament writers almost never develop any doctrines about Christ as part

71]

of systematic theological reflection. Rather, they interpret Jesus (technically this is called "Christology") by showing what his life (history) means for theirs. At the Lord's Supper, the believers do not remember Jesus simply to keep their memory alive but in order to vivify their commitment. The Bible, then, is united by its insistence that the decisive events of the past must be told in such a way that God addresses the reader and summons him to obedience within the community.

CHAPTER

MEETING GOD HISTORICALLY

4

THE VALIDITY OF THE BIBLE stands or falls on what it says about God's will for man. The authority of the Bible does not come from the fact that it has preserved valuable sources for the historian but from the way it interprets God's will and work. In other words, the authority of the Bible rests on the way it theologizes—the way it interprets *theos*, God. Chapters Four and Five explore the way the Bible speaks about God.

Thou or It?

• First we notice the language the Bible uses for God. The Bible talks about God as if he were a man. From beginning to end, from one stratum of tradition to another, it uses anthropomorphisms. For example, God planted a garden (Genesis 2:8,9); he loves one and hates another (Malachi 1:2 f., Romans 9:13); he becomes angry (Exodus 4:14, Revelation 19:15). The Bible even mentions parts of his body: he has eyes, nostrils, mouth, ears, face, arms, hands—even a posterior!

Admittedly this is symbolic, but so is all language. What is important is that the Bible insists on symbolizing God in human terms. Although the Bible says man is created in the image of God, it is clear that biblical language about God is created in the image of man. Therefore some readers have simply inferred that man has actually created God in his own image. Such a conclusion is more clever than true.

Actually, using terms taken from human experience to talk about God does not make the Bible distinctive, for all religions do this. What is unique is that this "humanization of God" in the language about him stands side by side with a relentless rejection of every real image of God. The imagery of God in human terms saturates the Bible; at the same time the Bible repudiates every image of God in wood, stone, or metal (Exodus 20:1-6, Isaiah 44:9-20, Mark 13:14 f., I Thessalonians 1:9 f.). True, the Israelites did, from time to time, use images of God in worship (Exodus 32, I Kings 12:25-33, II Kings 21:1-18). But this shows that it is important to distinguish between Israelite religion and Old Testament faith, between what the people did and what the Old Testament writers say they should have done.

It is clear that the biblical writers rejected material representations of God, called idols. It is equally clear that they used human imagery to do so. They were not inconsistent; but, knowing that no particular image can really represent God, they felt free to use almost every kind of verbal imagery. For example, Hosea spoke of God's cov-

[74

enant with Israel in terms of marriage. He could do so because at the same time he insisted God had no female consort, as the Israelites implied when they used fertility rites to worship him. Similarly, the biblical writers were not afraid to speak of God as Father because they have become convinced that God is not a male being. The Bible never speaks of the divine genitals, even though surrounding cultures emphasized them in fertility rites. Rather, the Bible uses the term "father" to express God's care and control. In the Bible, the "Fatherhood of God" does not express the notion that God is the sire of the universe or man, but that he is the sovereign patriarch of the household—that is, of the whole creation.

Thus the first thing we must note is that basically the Bible speaks of God as if he were a person, as one whom we encounter as Thou and not as It. Therefore the language derived from "I" and "Thou" is the most appropriate way for the Bible to talk about "Him."

Some readers of the Bible are offended by the idea of God as Thou. They cannot conceive of God in personal terms and cannot entertain the notion that he actually confronts them personally. They do not regard themselves as unbelievers; they simply cannot get beyond speaking of God as It.

Sometimes this takes sophisticated forms. Thus one may speak of God as a phenomenon by selecting a phenomenon or experience and capitalizing it; thus God is Power, Love, Spirit, Goodness, the Drift-of-history. There is no need to expand this list or to argue the appeal of this way of thinking about God. Another way to de-. personalize God is more subtle. One may use personal terms like Father without taking them seriously. Words like Father are used poetically like "Mother Nature" though the real, functioning concept of God may be highly impersonal, precisely like "Nature." One reason we have difficulty with personal terms for God is that our culture has become largely depersonalized. Consequently, talking about God in personal terms often does not communicate anything—it presents only a blur. It is possible that by reminding us of the personal character of the God-man relation, the Bible may help to prevent the total depersonalization of man.

Be that as it may, here are two fundamental modes of thinking about God. Actually, we do not need to repudiate the impersonal language altogether, because it is essential for thinking about God philosophically, especially if one probes to the ontological basis of the biblical message.[1] What is essential, however, is that we see clearly that the Bible does not do this, but persists in using personal terms and sees even impersonal phenomena like storms as signs that the intensely personal God is present (for example, Exodus 19:16-20, Psalm 29). Yet, seeing how the Bible

[1] One of the merits of Paul Tillich's book, *Biblical Religion and the Search for Ultimate Reality* (Chicago: University of Chicago Press, 1955), is the fact that it shows how ontological positions underlie the biblical statements and therefore cannot be avoided or denied by theology as a whole.

talks about God leads us to ask why it does so.

• The Bible speaks about God as Thou because the community experienced him as such. The Bible seldom theorizes about this but simply assumes it. Israel and the Church understood themselves to be confronted by One who spoke promise and demand, who involved them with himself in a covenant. Writers within such a community therefore used the language derived from personal relationships and encounters. They chose personal terms, not because after due consideration these appeared to be the most promising, but because they were convinced God made himself known as men do—by speech and action. A man as an anatomical specimen can be known by autopsy, but this tells us little about the man as a person. This must be known by understanding what he says and does. The Bible assumes this is equally true of God; it speaks of God as Thou because the community believes it has heard him and seen his work.

This is why the Bible never analyzes God. The doctrine of the Trinity, which does this for Christians by using categories drawn from Greek philosophy, is not stated anywhere in the Bible.[2] The kind of question which this doctrine answers is a legitimate concern, but the Bible does not talk about God in this vein. Instead, it speaks of God in terms of his relationships to the world

[2] The Bible does, however, raise the issues to which the doctrine of the Trinity addresses itself. See such passages as John 1:1-18, II Corinthians 13:14, Colossians 1:15-20, Hebrews 1:1-4.

and men, and these are expressed in personal terms because the community believes itself to be involved in such relatedness. The biblical writers do not take up the position of objective observers who report how God and man are getting along. Rather, they speak out of a sense of being involved, even if they speak of God in third person. They grapple with the theological issues from the point of view of the arena, not the press-box. For instance, Job is not interested in the problem of suffering as such but in answering the mystery of his experience; he does not ask so much for an explanation of evil as for an opportunity to take his case directly to God (Job 12:1-22, 23:1-17, 30:19-23). For the same reason, the "answers" to such issues do not come in the form of general statements so much as in terms of personal address (for example, Job 38:1-40:2, Jeremiah 15:15-21, II Corinthians 12:1-10). In a word, the Bible theologizes more in terms of personal conversations, even arguments between God and man, than in terms of analytical statements because it refuses to make "Him" into an "It" for study and observation. Instead, it insists on hammering out its understanding of God (expressible also in descriptive statements, to be sure) in confrontation with Him, with a Thou who talks back and asks questions of his own.

In the Bible, this communication (which can be called "the Word of God") takes two forms: direct communication by visions or speech, and indirect revelation through events which need interpretation. Even when God communicates

[78

directly, he speaks about himself only insofar as this is necessary to interpret what he will do or what he commands. Exodus 3:13-17 sets the pace for the whole Bible. When Moses asked God to identify himself, God replied with a statement which is neither a definition of deity nor a doctrine about God. God said he is the One who makes himself known as the One who makes himself known: I WILL BE WHAT I WILL BE, or as it is more commonly translated, I AM WHO I AM.

God said to Moses, "I AM WHO I AM." And he said, "Say this to the people of Israel, 'I AM has sent me to you.'" God also said to Moses, "Say this to the people of Israel, 'The LORD, the God of your fathers, the God of Abraham, the God of Isaac and the God of Jacob, has sent me to you': this is my name forever, and thus I am to be remembered throughout all generations. . . ."

Then follows the command to return to Egypt with the news that this I AM will liberate the people. In other words, God's self-disclosure is bound to historical events. When God reveals himself he never communicates information about himself. He never reveals "theology." What he reveals is his will and work, and both of these concern human history.

The other kind of self-disclosure, indirect revelation through historical events, has two foci: the recipients of the revelation and the events through which it occurs. That is, God reveals himself *to* particular people *through* particular events in their own history. We think of Moses in the situation of Israelite slavery in Egypt, the prophet Amos in his context of mushrooming injustice, Jeremiah in the midst of a collapsing society, the writer of Daniel in time of persecution, Paul in the act of persecuting the Church. The Bible reports each man's receiving a revelation which is uniquely his own. At the same time, it was through particular events and their meanings that the divine Thou addressed them. Both sides of the coin are important. The next chapter concerns the way God reveals himself by historical events. The rest of this chapter will show why the situation of the recipient is so important for the understanding of God.

How Does Historicity Affect Hearing?

• The term "historicity" has developed a double meaning. Usually it means simply factuality. Thus "the historicity of Moses" means the factuality of Moses, that there really was such a person. But the term has a more subtle meaning as well. In this sense, "the historicity of Moses" means that Moses was conditioned by his place in history. In other words, the idea of historicity commonly means that a person or an event *can be located* in history; the second meaning emphasizes that this person or event is *conditioned by the point where he is located*. Now, we are concerned with the second meaning.

We must recognize at the outset that we generally want timeless, unconditioned Truth-with-a-capital-T. Orthodoxies of all kinds often become

viciously intolerant because they claim their for-
mulations or creeds to be eternal Truth (drawn
up *at some time*, however!). Thus Christian Orthodoxy has insisted that the truth in the Bible is
eternal, that the vicissitudes of time and history
do not really affect it. Wherever this view dominates, there is little room for seeing the conditioned character of everything the Bible says. We
must be clear. We are not denying that there is
such a thing as eternal Truth, unaffected by human history; we are simply denying that any man
actually has such a truth, for eternal, unconditioned Truth exists only with God.

Without saying so, the Bible undergirds this
point. Biblical writers have no doubt, of course,
that God is eternally one God or that he is faithful to his own character. But its concern is not to
record eternally valid statements about him. Because it assumes God makes himself known both
at particular points in history and by means of
particular events, it recognizes that Israel's understanding of God and her understanding of herself
are interrelated. The Bible is, in effect, a result
of the dialogue between the community's self-
interpretation and its God-interpretation. Consequently, everything the Bible says about God
must be seen in the light of the situation in which
it is said. The Bible itself implies this, for instance, by prefacing the Ten Commandments
with a reminder that the God who commands is
the one who liberated the people from servitude,
and that the people are to obey him as a liberated
community (Exodus 20:1-17). In the same way,

the New Testament discusses the Church in the light of what God has achieved through Jesus (for example, I Corinthians 3:10-15, Ephesians 2:11-22); conversely, it speaks of God and Christ in the light of what the community has experienced (for instance, Romans 1:1-6, Hebrews 2:10-18).

• As we turn to specific biblical affirmations about God, it would be easy to restrict ourselves to those insights which are not problematic, like monotheism, in order to show the continuing relevance of the Bible. Unfortunately, such ideas stand side by side with concepts which embarrass us. Moreover, choosing ideas which we also affirm may actually obscure the real point under discussion—that everything the Bible says about God is historical understanding. Therefore, we focus on several ideas of God which may appear objectionable. We do not want simply to show that the Bible is inadequate in places, but to underline its historicity as a whole. First we select two areas where we have trouble with what the Bible says about God. Then we shall show how seeing these as historically conditioned can help us over the hurdle, and finally we shall ask how we are able to decide which statements about God we may affirm for ourselves.

The Bible says things about God which we find hard to believe. One concerns the problem of suffering. No one can deny that the Bible often says religion pays, and pays well. It also says irreligion brings doom. This is a basic theme in the Book of Deuteronomy. The authors put the whole history of Israel under this alternative:

If you obey the commandments of the Lord your God . . . then you shall live and multiply and the Lord your God will bless you. . . . But if your heart turns away . . . you shall perish (Deuteronomy 30:16ff.).

In the same way, Psalm 1 assures the righteous man that "in all that he does, he prospers." A similar view saturates the collection of Proverbs. On the other hand, everyone knows that innocent men do suffer while scoundrels prosper. Hence we simply cannot believe a flat statement which says God guarantees prosperity to the faithful, chaos to the unfaithful.

We also find it hard to believe what the Bible says about God's relation to war. Of all the repugnant ideas about God in the Bible, the notion that he is a God of war perhaps leads the list (for instance, Exodus 15:3, Numbers 21:14, Psalm 18:34, Isaiah 34:6). One particularly offensive story is found in I Samuel 15, in which God commands King Saul to wage a holy war, a crusade, against the Amalekites. The entire population and its property are to be annihilated. The story reports a complete victory for Saul. But when he spared the best specimens of the flocks, property, and the vanquished King Agag, God's spokesman, Samuel, pronounced doom for Saul and personally took the sword and "hewed Agag in pieces before the Lord in Gilgal." The story ends with the comment that "the Lord repented that he had made Saul king over Israel" in the first place! Nothing is gained by downgrading the horror of the story.

There are at least three major ways to come to terms with this kind of portrait of God. One is to claim that all such objectionable ideas are in the Old Testament and can be set aside simply for this reason. The Old Testament God is a God of wrath and war and the New Testament God is one of love and peace. This was Marcion's view, and it continues to attract support. But such an approach cannot endure close examination because this shows that the New Testament takes the Old for granted and builds on it.

Another way of dealing with the objectionable ideas of God is to speak of "progressive revelation." In this view, the Bible contains a developing concept of God ranging from primitive, crude, and lusty ideas to sophisticated and spiritual ones. The Bible thus marks the places mankind has been in its pilgrimage to spirituality. This view has the real advantage of recognizing that genuine development has occurred. However, it is too closely wedded to an evolutionary scale, to the notion that religious ideas are on an historical escalator. But it is far from clear that all older ideas were primitive while recent ones are advanced. Besides, this view assumes that the *idea* of God is the real concern of the Bible, and that by locating this emerging concept one has found what the Bible wants to say. Though the Bible is, of course, concerned to talk about God, it is not interested in purveying increasingly adequate

[84

concepts about him. As students of the phenomenon of religion, we are legitimately interested in
the developing sophistication of man's understanding of the divine, but this is not what the
Bible itself wants to get across. But the most
serious weakness of this outlook is that it tempts
us to think we have outgrown those parts of the
Bible which are early and unsophisticated (or
even offensive), and that we may take seriously
only those ideas of God which are congenial to
us. This often amounts to an aesthetic appreciation for an idea of God. When this happens, the
point the Bible wants to get across has been
missed.

A more adequate approach is to emphasize the
historicity of all concepts of God, including those
in the Bible. This means that the assurance of
Deuteronomy is understood in light of the original setting and not viewed from the vantage point
of sophisticated spirituality. In other words, our
total historical knowledge of Israel and the
Church should equip us to stand momentarily
with the writers in order to think with them about
the character and will of God. Concretely, this
means we must exert enough empathy to perceive what the Deuteronomist heard the divine
Thou say to him, a seventh-century B.C. Israelite.
When this is done, Deuteronomy's words are no
longer simply glib promises of heaven-sent
wealth for the righteous, but a daring attempt
to interpret the history of his people in the light
of God's concern for their obedience. Convinced
that God was not indifferent to what the people

did, he dared to write the history of the people as the story of God and Israel saying "Yes" and "No" to each other.[3] In the writer's day, this was an exciting risk. It still is, as anyone finds when he tries to tell the story of American history in the same way. In other words, the Deuteronomic account of Israel's life shows us how the divine Thou addressed the Deuteronomists through their history and at that point in their history.

This is why the historical-critical method of studying the Bible is important, for it enables us to grasp what it actually meant to live as an Israelite in a given era. The more accurately we reconstruct the history of Israel and the Church, the more precisely we can see how the men of the Bible understood themselves to be addressed by the divine Thou.

Approaching the biblical understanding of God in this way does not rule out recognizing that real "progress" has been made. Seeing the historical conditionedness of everything the Bible says does not mean ignoring the real development of Israelite sensitivity and sophistication. It does, however, allow us to see the older, less developed materials in as positive a light as possible. In this

[3] The Deuteronomists' total output includes the Books of Deuteronomy, Joshua, Judges, Samuel, and Kings. Each of these, of course, depends on earlier sources. For a recent, important analysis of the Deuteronomic material, see Gerhard von Rad, *Studies in Deuteronomy*, David Stalker, tr.—Studies in Biblical Theology No. 9 (Naperville, Ill.: Alec R. Allenson, Inc., 1953). A less technical treatment is found in G. E. Wright & R. H. Fuller, *The Book of the Acts of God*—Anchor Book (Garden City: Doubleday & Co., 1960), pp. 99-135.

way, the older, more brutal parts of the Bible may still communicate valid insights—even to us.

At this point, it is helpful to return to the story of Saul, Agag, and Samuel. To understand the story appropriately, we must note three presuppositions of the situation. (a) The Amalekites were an ancient enemy which had harassed the Israelites for generations (Exodus 17, Judges 6). (b) Tribal warfare was a normal state of affairs (I Samuel 14:47-52) just as business competition is in our day. (c) A god's power was commonly judged by the measure of success his people had in war and by the size of territory they managed to control (Judges 11:22-24). Therefore, the continual harassment by the Amalekites seemed to mock the divine commitment to Israel in the covenant.

In this light, the story's import can emerge more clearly. The key is Saul's disobedience to .God's command to wage a holy war of complete annihilation.

And he [Saul] took Agag the king of the Amalekites alive, and utterly destroyed all the people with the edge of the sword. But Saul and the people spared Agag, and the best of the sheep and of the oxen and of the fatlings, and the lambs, and all that was good, and would not utterly destroy them: all that was despised and worthless they utterly destroyed. (I Samuel 15:8f.)

Thus the holy war became a usual orgy of looting; despite the command that there was to be no personal benefit, Saul and his troops could not pass up the booty. Hence, the story says three things. One, this was not to be a normal tribal war with plenty of pillage. God actually summoned Saul to a new concept of holy war. Two, Saul disobeyed because he could not take this step; furthermore, he fled his responsibility:

And Saul said to Samuel, "I have obeyed the voice of the Lord, I have gone on the mission on which the Lord sent me, I have brought Agag . . . and I have utterly destroyed the Amalekites. But the people took of the spoil . . . the best of the things devoted to destruction, to sacrifice to the Lord your God in Gilgal." (I Samuel 15:20f.)

Finally, Samuel's response was revolutionary: "To obey is better than sacrifice." There is no substitute for obedience, not even a religious act. This is why Samuel took the sword himself, for he was committed to bringing to pass what the Lord commanded. So he "hewed Agag in pieces before the Lord."

Seen in its own setting, the story is no longer simply a repulsive story of a bloodthirsty God. In its native habitat the story shows a stern and sophisticated understanding of God's command and of the seriousness of obedience. The blood and fury are still there, and still offend us, but we see more than the gore. The Bible must be read in this way because this shows that the divine Thou addresses men *where they are*, summons them to unexpected aspects of obedience and responds as a real Thou to their disobedience. This is a basic pattern found again and again in

[88

the Bible. So we underscore what was said earlier: the Bible does not present us with eternal doctrines about God but with a way of seeing how God spoke to men in their histories. Thus it raises the question whether he still speaks this way.

Must I Believe Everything It Says About God?

Having seen the kind of statements about God which appear objectionable, and having seen how historical understanding enables us to see positive merit in them, we must still face the question, What shall *we* do with these ideas today? Because a story like that in I Samuel 15 is in our Bible, must we accept its idea of God's will as our own? To be sure, many Americans seem to be willing to launch a crusade against "atheistic communism" (Saul's war might be called a preventive war!). But, if we finally shake our heads and say, "No, this is not an adequate picture of God's will and character," we should know why we have come to such a conclusion.

To begin with, we must see that it is necessary to make distinctions within the Bible, for not everything in it has the same weight. Certain parts are more adequate expressions of God's will and character than others. Actually, everyone makes such distinctions whether he realizes it or not. True, there are those who say, "I believe the Bible from cover to cover, and the cover too because there it says 'Holy Bible.'" But such a person fools himself because it is simply impossible to give every statement in the Bible the same authority. The real question is not whether one should make distinctions between what is more adequate and what is less; the real question is the standard by which distinctions are made.

To this question, we make three comments. First, the standard ought to be appropriate to the Bible. Many Christians read the Bible through the eyes of the creeds. This, among other things, is what creeds are for. Others use a general definition of God, like "God is Love," to select those parts of the Bible which are decisive. Others operate with a general principle, like "the Fatherhood of God and the Brotherhood of man," and use those passages which contribute to this idea. But all these approaches suffer from the same defect—they cannot take seriously enough the historical character of the Bible. In its own way, each of these methods weighs biblical ideas on the scale of abstract statements. When a story like I Samuel 15 is read in this way, it turns out to be fairly useless, except as a negative illustration.

Instead of measuring historical ideas of God by nonhistorical standards (as creeds, principles, and definitions tend to be), one ought to measure what the Bible says by using a historical norm. The Bible itself shows how this is to be done. In the Old Testament, the exodus from Egypt is the pulse-giving event. Generation after generation, the interpreters of Israelite faith went back to this event and addressed their own times in its light, and thereby reinterpreted the exodus itself as well. The New Testament did the same, but used Jesus as the touchstone instead. Thus the Bible uses one historical event as the clue to others, and thereby hammers out its concepts of God on the same anvil.

• Jesus the Christ is the standard by which Christians determine what is mandatory. Since Christians believe that Jesus did not replace the Old Testament as Marcion claimed but became its fulfillment, he is the lens through which Christians read the whole Bible. Orthodoxy has always insisted, and correctly, that Christ is the center of Scripture. Regrettably, it did not see that Jesus Christ is also an historical criterion.

This central conviction has not always been stated properly. Traditionally, people simply said that the Old Testament predicts Christ. Therefore every conceivable passage (and many others as well) was combed to find predictions. Prophecies were found wherever the interpreter's ingenuity located them. Consequently, studying the Old Testament was like dowsing for water with a willow stick. This kind of study should have ended long ago. True, the New Testament itself sometimes uses the Old Testament in this way. But precisely this way of reading the Old Testament illustrates the historicity of the New Testament writers, for in their day this was the accepted way of reading Scripture. On the other hand, the New Testament writers are not nearly so literal and arbitrary in this matter as sometimes is claimed.

Be that as it may, we should not stop seeing

Jesus as the link between the Testaments and the lens by which both are read. When the whole matter is thought through again, it becomes clear that it is not nearly so important to find Christ in the Old Testament as it is to find the Old Testament in Christ. That is, what is decisive is not finding predictions of Jesus but locating ways in which Jesus gives concreteness to certain emphases of the Old Testament.

To begin, Jesus made the Old Testament the foundation of his mission. He did this by intensifying its demands for total obedience to God alone. If he appears critical of contemporary Judaism, as in Mark 7, it is because he reasserts the fundamental axioms of the Old Testament in a radical way. Thus Jesus said, "You have heard . . . 'An eye for an eye. . . .' But I say to you, Do not resist one who is evil." (Matthew 5:38f.) This does not simply set aside the Old Testament law of retaliation, but deepens its intent. Originally, the "eye for an eye" was not a green light for revenge but a stop light marking the limits of retaliation. Jesus deepened this original concern for the guilty by prohibiting all retaliation. By intensifying the Old Testament, he confirmed it. According to Matthew, Jesus said he came "not to abolish . . . but to fulfill" the law. Whether the precise wording is from Jesus' own lips or not, it clearly expresses the thrust of his mission as a whole.

Another way Jesus gave concretion to the Old Testament is by going to Jesusalem knowing he would probably seal the decision with his blood.

Three times Mark reports the so-called "passion predictions" (Mark 8:31, 9:30-32, 10:32-34). Some of these phrases were shaped in the light of the events that transpired. Still, it seems clear that Jesus reckoned with his destiny and found a way to pursue it. His attitude toward suffering stands in close relation to the deepest moment of the Old Testament insight on the problem, the poems of Second Isaiah (especially Isaiah 53). Scholars debate the extent to which Jesus deliberately shaped his demeanor to this pattern, but in any case his life fits it. In this way, he fulfilled the Old Testament and gave concreteness to its profoundest insight.

But what makes Jesus' relation to the Old Testament decisive is his resurrection. Without this, Jesus remains an enigma or a failure, despite his close relation to the Hebrew Bible. After all, what difference would it make how Jesus stood in relation to the Old Testament if God had not vindicated him? We must not forget that those who helped to do away with him were the recognized interpreters of the Hebrew Bible.

To emphasize the resurrection does not mean that we rummage through the Old Testament to find predictions of it. It means that we draw certain inferences from the fact that of the three men who died on Good Friday afternoon, only one was raised from the dead. By resurrecting Jesus, God put his stamp of approval on him and his mission. Since his life was dominated by the Old Testament, the vindication of Jesus means that the basis of his life has been ratified also.

We may illustrate this by a hypothetical situation. Assume three students are summoned to the Dean's office. Each is in difficulty with the police: one for drunken driving, another for disorderly conduct after a football game, the third for getting caught in a downtown disturbance over segregated facilities. As far as the police are concerned, all are guilty. But if the Dean were to nominate one of them for the Founder's Medal, he would be validating this student's conduct despite the opinions of the police. Similarly, on Easter God validated the mission of Jesus. This is what makes his life, and its basis, so important.

Specifically, how does Jesus' life help us to read the Old Testament? The simplest way to illustrate this is to return to Saul, Agag, and Samuel again. To begin with, when Jesus' life is seen as a whole, it is clear that obedience to God dominates it. Hence, the seriousness with which obedience is taken in I Samuel 15 is validated by Jesus' own career. Moreover, Samuel's dictum, "To obey is better than sacrifice" is also confirmed by Jesus because he made the same point in his own context (for instance, Mark 7:1-23, Matthew 5:21-24). Still, both the Sermon on the Mount and the character of his life point away from God's command to Saul—holy war. Hence, this command cannot be normative for Jesus' followers. On the other hand, if Jesus had been a military Messiah who avenged the Jews by leading a crusade against Rome, then the

[94

command for holy war would have been validated and given definitive sanction by the Messianic general. Since Jesus refused this role, we refuse to believe holy wars are God's will. The medieval Crusades against the Turks show the peril of not reading the Bible properly.

In other words, Jesus as the Christ is the gauge by which every disclosure of God's will is measured. What is not consistent with this standard cannot be normative for the Christian. Historical study alone cannot solve all the problems we have with the Bible. True, approaching the Agag story historically permits us to see it in a proper light, and this is basic. But understanding what it meant *then* does not by itself show the role it can have *now*. For the Christian the ultimate mandate must always come from Jesus and the implications of what God achieved through him. In other words, even with the indispensable insights provided by the historical method, when the modern Christian reads the Old Testament through the lens of Christ, parts of it become Christianized. Thus he does in his way what the first Christians did in theirs. After all, this is what it means to have a Scripture in a community of faith.

But even though in the light of Jesus we may not accept a particular biblical command as an adequate disclosure of God's will *now*, we must not conclude that God did not reveal himself *then* in just such terms. In fact, we must emphasize that this kind of revelation occurred *to them in their history*. In this light, we must also say

95]

that when the Christian reads the Bible through the lens of Christ, he listens for the Word of God in *his own time*. This is what it means to meet God historically.

HISTORY AS HIS STORY

THE BIBLE CLAIMS God discloses himself in history. Having seen how the situations of the recipients of the revelation affect the disclosure of God, we now turn the coin over and ask how history reveals God. Three matters will be considered. First, we need to sharpen our conception of what history is; then we shall compare the historian's way of presenting history with the way the Bible deals with it, and finally we shall look at what the biblical mode of telling history implies.

How Does the Past Become History?

• The historian wants to learn what happened. But "what happened" is not an adequate concept of history. To begin with, history is not the sum of everything that happened. Many things occur which are not really eligible for "history" because they have no significant relation to meaningful happenings. For example, during a football game, things may occur on the field which turn out to be irrelevant to the course of the game. The cameras record the entire action, but the history of the game is those actions, movements, and plays which contribute to the outcome. In fact, some frames of the film can be edited out with no loss because what they record is accurate but irrelevant. Moreover, some frames will become significant only in retrospect, after one sees how a certain play succeeded because of what happened earlier on one end of the line. Without such consequences this action would not really be part of the history of the game. In other words, history is more than happenings: history is happenings in meaningful relationships.

Another reason that we must distinguish between history and mere happenings is that the past does not present itself as history. The meaningful relationships are not built-in. History is the result of bringing order to the data, of relating it to general knowledge and to our tradition. The archeologist, for instance, unearths broken pots, a shred of fiber from a mat, a thick layer of charred matter, a rabbit bone. To these data he brings his total understanding of primitive cultures. When he relates these findings to those from similar excavations and to other knowledge, these remnants of the past become genuine history.

We also distinguish between the past and history because we must remind ourselves that there is no history in which the historian does not participate. History exists only where the past has meaning. "Pastness" exists as a stubborn datum; "history" exists only where the past is related to the present. It can be an unconscious relationship, such as the way most people are unaware that their notions of the soul are related to ancient Greek ideas; it can also be related by deliberate effort, as in the historian's work of recovering and understanding Mycenaean civilization.

• In this light, we can clarify the role of the historian. Basically he aims to understand the past as history, to view it as an intelligible past. This means he first finds out what happened: earthquakes, wars, marriages, works of art, waves of fear. But the historian does not want simply to catalogue the past; he wants to understand it, to interpret it so that it is intelligible for someone else. To do this, he must become involved in his work. Little participation is required if one is working on chronological problems, but much more is demanded if the historian is trying to make the period "come alive," trying to "get the feel of" the era, or "get inside" a figure like Peter the Great. On this level, the historian inevitably imports his own historicity into the material; as his own situation changes, he modifies his understanding of history. We see this clearly in the ways the Civil War has been interpreted. In fact, we can speak of the "history of the histories of the Civil War."

Everything we have said applies to biblical history as well. Our own modernity is revealed by the way we understand the Bible, just as the biblical writers' own times are revealed in the ways they viewed their history. Thus, for example, the historical situation of the writer of John's Gospel is revealed in the way he writes about Jesus, and our historical situation is disclosed in the way we write about John's Gospel and Jesus. This is why no perfectly objective biblical interpretation is possible. The student of the Bible who is sensitive to the problem will discipline his judgments so that they are not *unduly* swayed by his own standpoint. This is the art of making a truly critical judgment.

What If the Historian Tells It Differently?

The critical historian has demonstrated that basically the Bible may be regarded as a reliable historical source when it is properly understood. Every book dealing with archeology and the Bible makes this point; in fact, the real danger may be that this point has been overstated. Be that as it may, our purpose here is to outline the consequences historical study has for the authority of the Bible.

• In particular, we now return to our earlier observation that strictly historical study does not always validate the historical narratives in the Bible (such as the Israelite invasion of Palestine, commented upon later). In discovering this, many students find themselves in a dilemma: if, by granting that the historian's work must stand or fall on its own merit, they follow the historian's conclusions instead of the biblical account, they appear to repudiate the Bible. Biblical statements about astronomy or genetics need not be taken so seriously because these are not the Bible's concern. But since the Bible hangs its case on history, so to speak, it appears that the authority of the

Bible is jeopardized if the historian concludes that a particular event was not what the Bible says it was. This is a serious problem, and to it we address four considerations.

(a) We should conclude neither that the Bible is untrue nor that the historian is "destroying the Bible." These opposite conclusions flow from the same assumption—that the validity of the Bible hangs on the literal veracity of its statements. The liberal is just as much a literalist as the fundamentalist; but because he starts with different assumptions, he comes to different conclusions. Both assume that the Bible really intends to give an account which will pass the test of the modern historian's critical judgment. Because the fundamentalist assumes that the Bible is flawless in every detail he concludes that if the historian's work does not validate the Bible, it is destroyed or the historian must be wrong. Because the liberal assumes the Bible is a compend of religious literature of varying worth to begin with, he is often relieved when the historian's conclusions suggest that he need not believe it anyway. But both assume that the decisive criterion for the Bible is whether or not it will pass the historian's screen test; both are closed to the Bible's own way of dealing with history.

(b) When the historian reconstructs what happened or what was actually said, he is not trying to correct the Bible. He is exercising his obligations as an honest student of the past. Regardless of his results, he is not attempting to substitute his critical reconstruction for the biblical narra-

101]

tive. For example, even if we grant that the reconstruction of the Israelite invasion of Palestine differs from what the Bible reports, no historian's description is made "Scripture."

(c) The historian's work does, however, throw into sharp relief the real character and intent of the biblical narrative. Just as we learn something important about Harold Ickes by comparing his diary with the historian's account of the Roosevelt Era, so we learn something about the biblical way of telling about Israel's invasion by comparing it with the historian's reconstruction.

Concretely, we should never have seen the biblical writer's concern to express and promote the fundamental unity of the tribes by portraying their past as one in which they all shared, had we not concluded that probably they were not all in Egypt together. Moreover, such a conclusion does not make the writer dishonest, for he was eminently right: in his day the tribes were one people and the heritage of one had become the heritage of all. This is what the unity of the tribes came to mean. One way of saying this was to tell the tradition of one as the story of all. Besides, the later unity was made possible by the exodus of some tribes from Egypt. Consequently, the unity of the tribes is seen as just as much the work of God as the deliverance from Egypt. Hence, the story of the early days of settlement in Palestine is told from the same perspective as the exodus. Both are told to say something else—that in this sequence of events God created his people and bound them to himself in the covenant.

The historian describes these events in precisely the same terms he would use to discuss the emergence of any nation in history. The historian and the Bible have two ways of talking about the same events. The historian has no tools by which he can make a critical judgment that Israel's history is the work of God. At the same time, the authority of the Bible hangs on whether its way of telling the story is valid. We shall return to this point.

(d) If the biblical account differs from a strict report of what actually happened, we must ask why such a difference emerged. Usually it is pointed out that the writer stands within his community and its traditions. This seems to absolve the writer because now an amorphous community is the "culprit." Actually, this is the academic way of peeling onions because no one really knows where to stop. In any case, we should not hold a grudge against the community for "twisting the facts." Rather, we should ask why the "facts" were reported this way, or for that matter, why they were told at all.

• It is convenient to deal with the question by restricting ourselves to the problem of Jesus. First, we ask why we have four different accounts of his life. These four accounts simply cannot be completely harmonized without an abundant supply of imagination. The Gospels present different interpretations of Jesus. This is why the critical historian of his life must disengage him from the

103]

reports. As a matter of fact, modern study of Jesus' life is a series of variations on a fundamental theme announced in the eighteenth century: "We are justified in drawing an absolute distinction between the teachings of the Apostles in their writings [the Gospels] and what Jesus himself in his own lifetime proclaimed and taught." [1] Even though today few scholars would go this far, all historians of his life assume a distinction may have to be made. But this possibility must not be made the absolute starting point, so that one assumes the Gospels are distortions to be corrected wherever possible; nor can it be ruled out simply because the Gospels are in the Bible. But the real question remains: Why did the Church modify the traditions about Jesus? Why didn't it transmit "the facts" with complete accuracy?

Actually, we need to know *why* the Church remembered Jesus before we understand *how* it did so. The Church did not preserve the memory of Jesus for the sake of historians, not even for the sake of Christian historians. Rather, *the Church remembered the words and deeds of Jesus because they were useful in its life.* For example, Mark's Gospel, probably written in Rome around A.D. 65-70, reports what Jesus said about Jewish food laws (Mark 7:1-23). Why should Roman Christians be interested in such matters thirty-five years later? Mark and the Roman be-

---

[1] H. S. Reimarus, quoted by Albert Schweitzer, *The Quest of the Historical Jesus*, W. Montgomery, tr. (London: A. & C. Black, 1910—reprinted 1952), p. 16.

lievers valued this tradition because it helped them to face analogous problems of their own. The Church did not remember Jesus' words as those spoken by a Galilean teacher before he was martyred. Rather, the community believed that Jesus was the Lord because God raised him from the dead. Hence, they *treasured the tradition because in it they continued to hear the living Lord speak.* In time, only those teachings and deeds of Jesus were remembered which were most important. The rest were forgotten.

Moreover, the teachings were modified as they were used. Phrases were omitted, sayings were condensed or elaborated in order to make the point clear in the new situation. Thus the tradition was tailored so that it could fit the ongoing life of the Church. Besides, translating from Aramaic to Greek brought its own kind of changes. To have passed on these traditions without any change would have meant that they were regarded as verbal talismans, as sacred objects with a built-in power of their own. The medieval Church may have had priests who recited the mass without understanding its Latin, but the early Church had no such attitudes about the words of Jesus.

The changes, then, are actually the footprints of relevance. When the historian shows how the words of Jesus have been modified as they were used, or how the stories about him were adapted by the Church, he is not writing an indictment against the Church's integrity. He is really tracing the history of relevance. He is allowing us to

105]

look in on the early Church as it kept relating its
life to the life of Jesus. In a way, every preacher
who relates the words of Jesus to his own congregation continues this process.

In other words, the tradition was adapted as
it was used because the Church believed Jesus'
history continued to be a means by which God's
will was known. Had the tradition been transmitted without any modification at all, the
Church would have tacitly admitted that God
did not continue to say anything through Jesus'
history. But by modifying what they remembered, they showed they believed God kept on
addressing the Church when it recalled Jesus'
life and related it to their own. As a matter of
fact, once this assumption is surrendered, there
is little religious reason for saying that the Gospels are Scripture.

We can see how the Church used the stories
of Jesus in the account of the calling of the disciples (Mark 1:16-20). Taken literally, it is an
incredible historical narrative, for here four fish-
ermen simply abandon their work to follow a man
whom they had never seen before. In fact, two
of them walked off and left their father sitting in
the boat! The historian usually supplies the missing links: the men had met Jesus before and
there probably was more conversation than Mark
reports: "Follow me, and I will make you become
fishers of men." Such reconstruction is probably
valid. Still, this is not what Mark wants the
reader to see. He wants to make two things clear:
that Jesus is the Son of God who summons men

to follow, and that a disciple is one who is willing to abandon everything, including profession and father, to do so. In other words, the story is a highly stylized narrative which conveys the significance of Jesus and the appropriate response. The story is not told simply to report how Jesus got his first followers but to remind the Church who Jesus is and what they must do. The story is historical in the sense that it reports an actual event. It is not historical in the sense of describing accurately what happened. The event is used as a summons to faith. The report has been shaped into a sermon.[2] In one way or another, this is true for the whole Bible.

How Is Human History the Story of God?

• When the Bible tells history, God is the "leading man." This is in keeping with the conviction that God is the divine Thou. Throughout the Bible, history is *his story*. Not only is this assumed, but the prophets, poets, narrators, and apostles assert it. A few random selections illustrate the point. The prophet Amos asks, "Did I not bring up Israel from the land of Egypt . . . ?" (Amos 9:7f.). The entire 136th Psalm is a litany in which the congregation responds with "for his steadfast love endures forever" while the "cantor" recites the acts of God in history: he brought Israel from Egypt, led the people in the

[2] For a similar analysis see Günther Bornkamm, *Jesus of Nazareth*, Irene and Fraser McLuskey with James M. Robinson, trs. (New York: Harper & Brothers, 1960), pp. 144-148.

wilderness, slew famous kings, gave the land of Palestine. The narrator of the Book of Judges repeatedly shows how God responded to Israel's faithlessness such as when he says, "And the Lord sold them into the hand of Jabin king of Canaan" (Judges 4:2). The apostles sound the theme of Christian preaching by announcing that God had done mighty works through Jesus of Nazareth (Acts 2:22ff.).

This conviction also· influences the way the stories are woven together. Thus the creation of the world and the story of man's sin are told as a prelude to the story of Israel in order to show that the divine Thou operating in Israel's history actually began his work when he created the heavens and the earth and that he concerned himself with human obedience as early as the Garden of Eden. Likewise, the Gospel of Mark begins with Jesus' baptism and temptation (1:1-13) to show that Jesus is the Son of God on whom the Spirit came. The Spirit then drove him into the wilderness where Satan tested him. This sets the stage by telling the reader that the story of Jesus is really the story about God's power launching an attack on Satan through Jesus.

• At the same time, however, the Bible is convinced that the human actors in the drama have real responsibility. At no point are men seen as mere puppets on divine strings. The Bible never thinks it must choose between human and divine actors. Rather, it sees men's lives, speeches, wars, as instruments of divine action.

For example, Judges 4 and 5 report an episode

of the era before the Israelite monarchy. The whole period is interpreted as a cycle of Israelite disobedience, divinely sent oppression by enemies, Israelite pleas for divine help, God's response by effecting successful campaigns against oppressors. In Judges 4, the current enemy is Jabin, whose general, Sisera, commands an "armored division" of 900 iron chariots. The subjected Israelites are still without this precious metal. The story begins with the prophetess Deborah's inspiring Barak to lead a revolt. The decisive battle occurred on a plain not far from modern Haifa. A cloudburst turned the land into a sea of mud so that the heavy chariots were bogged down in the mire, and the swollen stream apparently cut off the escape route. So the Israelites won decisively. Thus runs a historian's reconstruction. But note how the Book of Judges understands it: "And the Lord subdued Sisera and all his host"; "So on that day God subdued Jabin . . . before the people of Israel." The writers do not suggest that the Israelites remained in their tents while God won the battle (by commandeering the weather). What they want to say is that the victory, in which the Israelite guerillas doubtless gave a good account of themselves, was really God's victory for them. Judges 5 is a ballad-like poem which celebrates the victory in the same vein.

In this account, which is by no means unique in its outlook, the writers do not speak of divine action in history as one more factor among others. The Bible's statements about God's action in human affairs do not stem from an astute analysis of historical causes. When the modern historian talks about the causes of the Civil War he is not speaking in the same vein as the Bible when it says the war with Jabin was caused by God's response to Israel's sin. Similarly, in speaking of the great battle, the historian can only say that on that day "it rained"; the Israelite, on the other hand, believed "God rained," therefore it was his victory. In other words, the biblical way of talking about God as the chief actor in this history is not a way of locating decisive historical causes ascertainable by empirical study. Rather, it is a way of saying that the historical events have moral meaning.

One of the great passages in the Old Testament asserts that the militantly aggressive Assyria was actually God's tool (Isaiah 10:5-19) even though the Assyrians worshiped other gods and would themselves be doomed for their arrogance and cruelty. No analysis of the contemporary eighth-century B.C. power politics in the Near East would require such a conclusion. No assessment of the causative factors in Assyrian foreign policy will include alongside others (or even at the head of the list) this one—that the God of Israel was at work, using the Assyrian armies for his own ends. We may catch something of the Bible's way of talking about the acts of God by daring to say that the reason the Germans never invaded the British Isles in World War II was because God did not allow it. Such a statement by no means rules out all the specific policy decisions and

[110

their historical causes within the German High Command; but it does require the reader to decide whether this frustrated plan, which doubtless would have changed the course of all subsequent modern history, has any meaning in the ultimate scheme of things, or is just a fluke of history.

In other words, biblical statements about God's acts in history express convictions about what history ultimately means; they do not select the divine cause among all the causes in the situation. If the latter were true, then God's action in history would be available to good historical study. But one cannot determine which cause of Hitler's failure to invade Britain, for example, was the divine element in history. Saying that God prevented it is rather a way of talking about the meaning of the whole event.

Moreover, seeing God's acts in history is possible only to the eye of faith. This is not because such an interpretation is an obscure secret, but because it springs from a conviction about what history ultimately means. When faith in God faces the question of whether history has any ultimate meaning, it says that God is at work in the course of events. The biblical writers do not face our kind of question concerning causation, historical or natural. Therefore they do not hesitate to say directly that God did this or that. Our difficulty is that we assume these statements talk about *our* understanding of causes and effects. When we read the Bible, then, it is important that our kind of question should not stand in the

111]

way of seeing their questions and answers. Seeing the way the biblical writers deal with the question of whether historical experience is meaningful may offer us clues to the way we might face the enigmas of our own history.

• The technical term for a story which tells about the actions of the divine on earth is "myth." In other words, the biblical way of talking about history is mythological.

We must shave some of the fuzziness off this concept. As a starter, we may say that we do not always have to choose between myth and history because the contrast is not simply between fiction and fact.[3] We cannot accept the notion of myth as a story that is not true, for this is too limited a definition. It is more correct to say that myth and history can be two modes of talking about the same event. The historian's description of Jabin's defeat and the biblical account illustrate

[3] A basic danger in dealing with myths and mythic language is literalism. Stories of satyrs, demons, and demigods may not have been taken so literally in their original settings as we positivistically minded moderns often assume. Such stories were perhaps told not simply for their entertaining content but to express dimensions of understanding which eluded more prosaic forms of communication. Reinhold Niebuhr has formulated important insights regarding myth in *An Interpretation of Christian Ethics* (New York: Harper & Brothers, 1935)—reprinted in paperback in Living Age Books series (New York: Meridian Books, 1956), pp. 31ff. and especially Chapter 3 in which he deals with the concept of sin. Similarly, suggestive comments are made by Nicolai Berdyaev, *Freedom and the Spirit,* Oliver Fielding Clarke, tr. (London: Geoffrey Bles: The Centenary Press, 1953), pp. 69-74.

this distinction very well. In the same vein, the historian speaks of the Israelite invasion of Palestine, but the biblical writers talk about God's giving them the land, or keeping his promise to Abraham. We apply the term "myth" to this latter way of talking about the event without in any way denying that the Hebrews entered Palestine as invaders.

A second misconception of myth must be corrected. It is commonly said that myth is simply the pre-scientific mode of expressing meaning, that myth is the language of early cultures before they developed adequate (analytical) categories of thought.[4] Clearly this conception is more accurate than one which simply sweeps myth aside as untrue fabrication, for obviously many ancient myths are vehicles of profound insight. Sometimes, however, this concept of myth becomes seriously handicapped, for occasionally people assume that science precludes myth and makes it altogether unnecessary. But this simply will not do. We cannot conclude that because mankind thought mythically before he thought scientifically, he no longer needs myth. Therefore it is better to speak of myth as nonscientific thought, and leave open the question whether or not a person can operate with both modes of interpreting reality. Certainly the Freudians have operated with myths, not merely with the Oedipus family

[4] The myths of the ancient Near East are given a very helpful treatment in this vein by H. & H. A. Frankfort, John Wilson, and Thorkild Jacobsen in *Before Philosophy* —Pelican Book (Baltimore: Penguin Books, Inc., 1949).

but with the self-made myth of the Id and the Superego. Their domains have also been mapped, much as the realms of demons once were. The point is that working with these mythological constructs allows the Freudian psychotherapist to deal meaningfully with a body of material and to interpret it in universal terms. This is precisely what myth intends, whether it be the myth of Oedipus (in connection with guilt) or the myth of Adam (in connection with sin).

The language of myth, then, is not an unfortunate left-over from the dawn of history, like the human appendix. Nor is mythic speech an option which one may or may not use, for there is no way to talk about ultimate, transcendent meanings without using mythic speech. True, one can speak of important meanings, such as the genuinely decisive meaning Karl Marx' *Das Kapital* has for modern history. But when we refer to ultimate meanings, we point to a dimension of reality which transcends history as a whole. We can avoid myth only by avoiding the problems of transcendent values and meanings. Besides, when these ultimate values and meanings center in the divine Thou, events which reflect these meanings may be spoken of as the deeds of God. To talk about God's acts is to speak mythologically. The Bible is filled with such language and is unintelligible without it.

• There has been much discussion over the fact that the Bible speaks of history in mythic language. One problem is that the particular form of mythic thought is grounded in the ancient world view in which the universe is a three-storied affair populated by invisible powers and beings. Our post-Copernican world has made this outlook impossible if taken literally. The question, however, is whether the biblical mode of reporting historical events went into the museum with the ancient world view.

Rudolf Bultmann, the German New Testament scholar, has answered with a loud "Yes." He has gone on to advocate interpreting the biblical mythology in nonmythological terms; what the Bible said in its (mythic) idiom he wants to say in our own (existential) terms. His word for this process of interpretation is "demythologizing." [5] He admits that it is not a good term because it is negative. Still, it is appropriate because Bultmann really wants to avoid talking in mythological terms because he says this makes the acts of God one more historical cause, and a cause which interrupts the normal flow of events at that.

A full evaluation of this proposal is out of the question here. Only two comments can be made. First, it is not at all certain that the Bible intends to speak of God's action as an interruption of history. This is certainly not the case in the story

[5] Bultmann's proposal is now available in Hans Werner Bartsch, ed., *Kerygma and Myth*, Reginald Fuller, tr. (Greenwich: Seabury Press, 1953)—reprinted in paperback (New York: Harper Torchbook, 1961). This volume contains also the first of an avalanche of literature on the subject. Bultmann himself restated his position in *Jesus Christ and Mythology* (New York: Charles Scribner's Sons, 1958).

of Jabin's defeat. Nor is it the way the crossing of the Red Sea is told. Exodus 14:21 reports ". . . the Lord drove the sea back by a strong east wind all night, and made the sea dry land, and the waters were divided." The writer does not think he must choose between the act of God and the blowing of the wind because he understands the wind as the act of God. How would the writer speak of this event in ultimate terms if he could not say "God drove the sea back"?

Even more important is the question whether Bultmann's proposal ought not to be reversed. Perhaps the real aim is not to "demythologize the message of the Bible" but to mythologize the outlook of the reader. The Bible intends to present the history of Israel, Jesus, and the Church as the story of God's work in the world, and to do so in a way that summons the reader to become part of the story. Instead of trying to interpret the Bible primarily in terms of the new possibilities which it presents to the individual man facing anxiety (a basic theme of existentialist interpretation), perhaps one ought to try to give man a framework within which he may understand his own history.

Part of our modern dilemma is that we have no overarching mythology. We try to find meaning in a mass of data which has been sterilized to remove the transcendent, the intangible, the mysterious. That is, we try to find adequate meaning in historical events as they are seen by the critical historian or the statistical student of society. The clue, however, to the meaning of our historical experience is not found in monographs but in myths. Besides, ours is not only the Atomic Age but the Atomistic Age as well. We have no real intellectual or spiritual universe: we have only specialties, private universes.[6] We lack a transcendent framework in which to interpret the course of our history as a whole. Put theologically, we lack a mythology to understand the meaning of our history.

Consequently, we may ask whether Bultmann has not seen a real problem but suggested the wrong answer. That the biblical myth cannot be revived in its original form is clear. What is not so clear is that we must therefore give up myth altogether. Perhaps the more appropriate alternative is "transmythologizing"—that is, following the analogy of trans-lation, perhaps we should work our way toward a modern mythology into which the biblical way of talking about God and history can be translated. The existentialist individualism has powerful appeal today because we have grown cynical about the ultimate meaning of history, or of anything for that matter. But it is doubtful if one's personal existence, or personal history, can have any meaning if history as a whole is merely sequence in a void. In our situation, then, perhaps the very fact that the Bible speaks of history in mythological terms may be a Word to us.

[6] This point is well made by Fred Denbeaux in *The Art of Christian Doubt* (New York: Association Press, 1960), Chapter One.

THE AUTHORITY
THAT COUNTS

6

CAN SUCH A BIBLE still be our Scripture? This is our fundamental problem. By emphasizing the ways the Bible is rooted in a variety of cultural situations we have, in effect, hammered on the theme of its relativity. Thus the issue has been drop-forged: can such a Book have real authority today? But first, we must see what we mean by authority.

What Kind of Authority Do We Really Have?

• The notion of "authority in religion" often offends people. For many, religious faith is a matter so intimate, so inward and intangible that the idea of authority seems crudely inappropriate. Religion is a matter of the heart and the spirit, they argue, and in such matters one should not speak of authority but of freedom. Does not the whole struggle for religious toleration show that the conscience of man must be free? From this vantage point, authority in religion suggests an ominous return to the kind of medievalism we can do without.

Two things may be said to such reluctance. One is that we are not talking about the authority of a power-center (church or state) to compel compliance or coerce convictions. Rather than rehabilitating institutional authority, we are seeking to rethink the possibility that the Bible might still be Scripture. That is, we are facing the question whether the Bible may still be a norm for personal faith and life.

The second point is that authority is simply inescapable. There are no completely autonomous men. Everyone is thoroughly dependent on others for information, attitudes, expectations. The scholar's device for admitting this is the footnote, but there is no way for a person to footnote his whole life. To a large extent, personality may be described in terms of interaction of various authorities such as community mores, home life, inner standards which emerge by reflection. The question is never: "Shall I have an authority?" but always "What authority shall be supreme?" Thus the matter really turns on whether a person has clarified the relative priority of his authorities. The problem of biblical authority concerns the role the Bible may have in this hierarchy.

• For some people the Bible has the authority of God himself. It is THE authority because for them it is the inspired, infallible Word of God. To the fundamentalist, the Bible is the one point where the relativity of human existence is broken since the Bible provides immediate access to God.

Frequently, this view will not shrink from saying that all the words in the Bible actually came from God himself. This is the logical conclusion of so-called verbal inspiration.

This kind of biblical absolutism cannot be accepted, for despite the assurance it can generate, such authority is neither possible nor permissible. (a) Two considerations show that absolute authority is not possible. To begin with, no one has an unconditioned access to the Unconditioned One. The finitude of man is not suspended when he reads the Bible, nor was it suspended when it was written. True, the common idea of how the Bible was inspired is perilously close to this notion. This popular notion is the ancient Greek idea that in the moment of inspiration the human personality was put into a kind of cold storage; or, to use the Greeks' own example, the person became as a flute, passively ready to play whatever was breathed into it. Everything we have said about the emergence of the Bible points in another direction. The fundamentalist view of the Bible is almost that of Mormonism which holds the Book of Mormon to be translated from specially revealed gold tablets which have long since vanished.

But even if we were to grant that the Bible is not conditioned by history, nothing significant would be gained because in any case the reader is. An historic reader of an absolutely trans-historical text does not really have absolute truth but only what his own historicity will allow him to have. It is the persistent failure of fundamen-

121]

talism to reckon with this which frequently makes it so arrogant, for it constantly assumes it has unconditioned knowledge of God's unconditioned Book. Even if we were to grant this for the Bible, we cannot do so for the readers. In all honesty, we must admit we have no access to God which is not conditioned by finitude and historicity. Fundamentalism, of course, has no monopoly on absolutism. It has often been observed that few people are more bigoted than "liberals" who feel themselves surrounded by closed minds. The liberal needs to see the historicity of his axioms just as much as the fundamentalist.

Second, absolute knowledge of God is impossible because of human perversity. This is what the Bible calls "sin." Before the impact of Freud's rediscovery of the irrational in man, one could talk about man without taking account of his persistent efforts to justify himself by conscious and unconscious means. Such naïveté is now impossible, for Freud taught us what the Bible knew—that the closer one gets to matters of decisive significance for the self (in this case, God), the less able he is to think disinterestedly. In fact, just the opposite is true. The closer one gets to the "nerve" of the self, the more devious are the efforts at self-protection and self-deception. Because the concept of God has decisive consequences for the self, no knowledge of God is free from this propensity.

Moreover, the tendency to tamper with the truth for the sake of the ego is utterly ubiquitous. It affects everyone, liberal and fundamentalist alike. Even if one were to say that the biblical authors were exempt from this tendency when they wrote, the readers are not. In other words, we have only that understanding of God and man which is affected by moral perversity. If the major sin of fundamentalism has been naïveté about the historicity of the Bible, the major sin of liberalism has been naïveté about the perversity of its readers.

Thus, no concept of biblical authority can ignore these twin modifiers of our knowledge of God: finitude (historicity) and perversity (sin). Together they make any doctrine of an unconditioned, absolute knowledge of God through the Bible (or anything else) a worthless definition hanging in a vacuum—admirable, but inaccessible to persons reading Bibles in history.

(b) Nor is biblical absolutism permissible theologically. The quest for (and insistence upon) the unconditioned nature of the Bible is really an attempt to reduce the leap of faith to a pedestrian hop. Frequently, the person who trumpets his claim that he believes so much *about* the Bible is actually incapable of *believing biblically*. Faith is reduced to affirming that certain propositions are true, including the proposition that the Bible is free from historicity. Where this occurs, faith is emasculated into mere confidence in reliable statements. Where historicity and relativity are excluded by definition, the risk of doubt is gone, and with it the possibility of faith. If one says he believes in God because he believes the Bible is a monolith of infallible truth, we may wonder if his real faith is a God or in a statement about the Bible.

Interestingly, the Bible sees the desire for absolute knowledge as the root of all sin. This is what tempted Eve to disobey.

But the serpent said to the woman, "You will not die. For God knows that when you eat of it [the tree of knowledge of good and evil] your eyes will be opened, and you will be like God, knowing good and evil." . . . The woman saw . . . that the tree was to be desired to make one wise. . . ." (Genesis 3:4-7)

The story says, in effect, that man must accept limited knowledge as an ingredient of his life.

The fact that absolute, unconditioned authority is not available to conditioned and contingent man must not lead us to conclude that no authority exists, for some kinds of authority do function. The real question is this: how can an ultimate authority (a Word from God) function through relative, historical, and contingent means? To put it concretely, the question is whether and how God communicates through a book like the Bible read by people like us.

How Does God Speak Through This Bible?

• It is fruitful to follow the grain of the Bible itself. We have seen that the writers report historical events in order to get the readers to share the author's understanding of it. By summoning the community to survey its history, the writer

[124

invited his readers to see God at work in it. He aimed for them to see what he saw.

Characteristically, the writers believed their work (Word) was "given" to them by God (for example, Jeremiah 1:1, Hosea 1:1, Joel 1:1. (This is doubtless true also of those who do not say so explicitly.) For this reason, some of the prophets report how God made himself known and laid his Word upon them (for instance, Isaiah 6, Ezekiel 1, Amos 7). Paul does the same thing in a different form (Galatians 1). In other words, having perceived how the divine Thou apprehended them in their own histories, and having grasped certain implications of this, they interpreted their situation (or the history of Israel) in this light. They placed themselves at the disposal of the Word they received so that their words might help the community to hear what they heard and to obey as they obeyed.

This means that if the reader is open enough to the intent of the writer to take him seriously, he risks making the response the author intends. The closer the reader follows the writer, the greater the danger that his own history will be illuminated by the light the author found, the greater the possibility that his own obedience will be ignited by the flame set going in the author's encounter with God. This is why sensitive Bible reading is an occasion for basic decisions about life. Reading the Bible can be dangerous because one risks exposing his life to the One the author met. The biblical author achieves one of his aims when the reader can say

125]

that God has met him too and has redeemed his history by giving him a mythology—that God has drawn him into the story of his work in the world. *The real authority of the Bible is its ability to bring about this encounter*. This role of the Bible in the encounter with God is the fundamental element of its authority.

• We must clarify the relation between the Bible and God in such an encounter. When a person affirms that as he read the Bible God addressed him, he frequently speaks of it as God's Word. He need not do so because of some rigid definition of the Bible but because in reading it he has been accosted by the Other One. As was outlined before, the biblical God is so intensely personal that one never meets him as an impersonal It, as one discovers the principle of gravity. Rather, when the reader is caught up in the perspective of the biblical writer, he encounters God as the divine Thou who addresses him Thou to thou.

We have emphasized the historical-critical method because this enables the reader to see what the writer is really trying to say and where he stands when he says it. One can surely be inspired without such knowledge, but one is never sure whether he has gotten the point that was actually intended. Only when the writer's work is understood can one look with him. The Church promotes critical study of the Bible in order to make this possible. Insofar as the critic helps the reader to find where the writer stands so that he can stand with him, the critic has been faithful to the intent of the Bible.

It can hardly be overemphasized, however, that nothing guarantees that understanding and empathy with the writer will produce an encounter with God. Critical study is not a recipe for religious experience. It can only help to make it possible; it can never make it inevitable, nor can anything else. This is because God is free to make himself known when and where he wills. He is not built into the text so that appropriate methods of study will locate him as a Geiger counter finds uranium.

Because one cannot guarantee that reading the Bible brings an encounter with God, it is not really correct to say simply that the Bible is the Word of God, for the word "is" does not point to a static relationship between God and the Bible as it does in the statement "The ink is black." God is not chained to the text but is free to make himself known through it or not to. It is therefore more accurate to say that the Bible *may become* the Word of God. In this way, we preserve what is really at stake in saying that the Bible is Scripture and we prevent Bible worship. Bibliolatry is sin because it makes the Bible as absolute as God. But by saying that under certain conditions, not controllable by the reader, God may address him through the Bible,[1] the

---

[1] The conception that God makes himself known through the Bible and that this disclosure is validated by God himself is decisive for Protestant thought. The classical phrase is "the inner witness of the Holy Spirit." We shall return to this point in the next chapter.

authority of the Bible is affirmed and the freedom of God is unimpaired. We must not barter
the freedom of God for the authority of the Bible.

• Next, we return to the reader who is addressed by God's Word and ask what this means
for him. When the reader risks looking with the
Bible and being apprehended by its God, he also
risks treating his own religious and social traditions the way the writer treated his. Suppose
one sees that the Israelite prophets understood
how the demand for relevant religion distorted
Israel's faith into the worship of God as a means
of guaranteeing prosperity. Armed with this insight, the reader can detect the same dangers in
our modern American interest in Religion-in-
general. He will be alert to the ways we use
Christianity to throw a cloak of divine approval
on the American Way of Life.

There is hardly a limit to the illustrations
which one could add. But this is not necessary
because the point is clear: the basic purpose of
the Bible is not fulfilled when one learns about
its outlook and contents, nor is it really fulfilled
when one is apprehended by God by reading it.
The fundamental purpose is fulfilled only when
the reader is drawn into the biblical community
and interprets his own situation under its impact.

This inevitably makes him a loyal critic—one
who is deeply committed to that element of the
tradition which is creative and constructive while
at the same time becoming an unflinching critic
of all those forces which threaten the heart of
the matter. In no case can he be content with a

[128

facile identification of tradition and the will of God, whether the traditions be those of "our church's way of doing things" (that is, mode of baptism, type of organization, or kind of liturgy) or community mores (that is, Southern customs in race relations or Yankee attitudes toward Italians). The reader who has been apprehended by the Word in the Bible knows that anyone who quotes the Bible to sanctify the *status quo* is prostituting the Scripture.

Of course, not every apprehended reader will hear the Word identically; nor will all hearers of the Word relate it to their setting in the same way. This is what the historicity of human hearing means. The fact that equally conscientious readers draw differing conclusions is no cause for despair. What is cause for despair is the fact that so often no concrete conclusions are drawn at all. But the Bible does not intend to be merely the medium of religious experience. It aims to get the reader beyond religious experience for its own sake so that it will occur for the sake of the community.

• Finally, the question of the relevance of the Bible is now in proper perspective. In the first place, if the real authority of the Bible lies in its being a catalyst for an encounter with God which cannot be guaranteed, then God himself determines which parts of the Bible are relevant. Since God is as free as he is sovereign, he is free to address the reader through any part of the Bible, even those parts with which we have serious troubles. The divine Word may address one

129]

reader as he follows Paul's analysis of the gospel in Romans 1-8, and yet another is left cold by the involved argument. In a sense, God's word is like lightning which cannot be predicted or controlled, precisely because it is *God's* Word.

In the second place, what is relevant is not simply what is useful. Much of the cry for relevance in religion is simply a thin veil for demanding that someone's program receive divine sanction. When this occurs, God is neither sovereign nor free; he has been demoted to a cosmic troubleshooter or a divine Dean of Men. But the relevance of the Bible is not to be measured simply by what we find useful to buttress our ideas or programs. The relevance of the Bible may consist precisely in its way of cutting across our notions, of arresting the flow of our assumptions. Frequently the most relevant passage is one which is least suspected.

Suppose a student couple have difficulties in marriage adjustment. What is relevant to their situation? The passages that deal with marriage and family? Perhaps. But usually, these will bypass a particular couple's problem. This does not make the Bible irrelevant, for what may be most relevant is not a Bible verse about womanhood or divorce but Paul's powerful analysis of the self in conflict as found in Romans 7. Here he states succinctly the agony of the person caught doing the things he detests. In a given household, this insight, unrelated at first glance, may speak a decisive word to a wife who alienates the man she really wants to love.

The point is that relevance in religion cannot be engineered without making God into a flunky. The Westminster Confession saw this when it began by saying "The chief end of man is to glorify God and to enjoy him forever." Modern man's passion for relevance at all costs turns this around so that it says "the chief end of God is to satisfy man and make himself useful forever." If the Bible can help us get out of this ego-centrism, it will be profoundly relevant—even if the point is made by stories about the bloody wars of Jehovah.

In the third place, when the reader takes up the biblical understanding of God and man and begins to understand his own situation in these terms, then the question of the social relevance of the Bible is solved. Particular kinds of ethical matters will be discussed in Chapter Eight. At this point we say simply that the real question is not whether the Bible is relevant for social problems but whether the reader has sufficient courage to follow the relevance he will see. He may hesitate because he wonders whether the summons he hears through the Bible is really God-sent.

Is the Encounter Authentic?

Since we have nailed the flag of biblical authority to the mast of an encounter with God, we cannot avoid asking how one knows he has encountered God. Is the appropriate symbol for Bible reading the telephone which connects two

131]

parties in conversation, or is it the radar which bounces back one's own signal?

The fundamentalist not only claims that the Bible is the Word of God himself but that he can demonstrate this. Ironically, the demonstration usually consists of quotations from the Bible! This may reassure those who do not really press the question, but it does not provide convincing argument for the issue itself.

Obviously, the problem of verification of religious knowledge cannot be treated here with any real adequacy. We must content ourselves with four suggestions which seem most indispensable:

• Verification of the encounter with God is neither possible nor permissible. Just as it is impossible to demonstrate the existence of God by either strictly empirical or logical evidence, so it is impossible to verify that a person has been confronted by God. At no point can the reader prove he has been apprehended by the divine Thou. He can offer data to support his conviction, but proof—evidence which permits only one conclusion—is something else. This may be disarming, but it is true.

If the reader *can* not prove that his encounter was with God, he *may* not prove it either. This is built into the human situation. The veil of ambiguity may not be lifted by mortals in history. Moreover, since the greater proves the lesser, the ultimate encounter (with God) cannot be proved by lesser encounters (with friends or public officials) offered as analogies.

Nonetheless, the conviction that God has spoken through the Bible can be communicated even if it is unprovable. Communication and proof are not the same thing. In communication, conviction is generated by more than logic, and sometimes by less—as everyone who has wooed and won a wife knows.

• For the person involved, the event authenticates itself. The reader cannot prove to another that his experience was an authentic encounter with God; he cannot prove it to himself either. But this is no flaw, for by definition there is no way of authenticating this event. This means, then, that the conviction that one is addressed by God is actually a confession and not a conclusion from evidence. The person apprehended affirms that One has spoken a Word to him which commands full obedience, that reading the Bible has brought a meeting with One whose presence is not debatable to the one addressed. When the biblical God steps out of the text and speaks to the reader, he "knows" he is in no position to contemplate an It but must answer Him. The Bible shows with remarkable consistency the self-authenticating character of such meetings: Moses, Amos, Isaiah, Paul, Peter.[2] Each man met by God learned that the encounter precluded

[2] See Exodus 3, Amos 7, Isaiah 6, Galatians 1, Acts 10. The dynamic of such encounters has been analyzed with fertile suggestiveness by Paul Minear in *Eyes of Faith* (Philadelphia: The Westminster Press, 1946). See especially Chapter 6.

133]

argument. In the moment of encounter, no one
asks God for his identity card.

• Nevertheless, theologians have not refused
to ask some questions about the encounter. The
traditional term for the immediate experience
of the divine is "the work of the Holy Spirit."
Ultimately, it must be said that the One who
elicits the conviction that God has spoken is the
Spirit of God himself. This may look like double
talk and obscurantism. It need not be, for every
assertion about human knowledge assumes that
at some point one has an immediate, almost in-
tuitive apprehension of truth. Without this, there
can be no meaningful discussion at all, for everyone assumes that he can make a judgment which
corresponds to reality. Hence the Christian insistence that it is God's Spirit which communicates truth is really a way of bringing this axiom
into focus by relating this immediate experience
of the Ultimate to the doctrine of God. This is
one of the issues in the doctrine of the Trinity.
For our problem, we may simply say that the
Spirit is the immediate Confirmer of the confession that we have met God. There is no way
to get behind this.

• The reader who believes God addressed him
finds that God spoke to others also. Consequently,
the Word of God creates a community of the
addressed, a community of those who are drawn
together for mutual clarification and interpretation of what they have heard. This is the Church,
and it is created by the Word, even though the
Church produced the Bible; in fact, the Church

produced it because it heard the Word and wanted others to hear it also. This is why the Bible has such an important place in Christian worship.

But the Church is not only the consequence of the Word but a criterion for it. That is, the community functions as a control over what may be considered "Word." The Church knows that not everything claimed for God's Word can be accepted as such, despite the convictions of its advocates. By its own accrued consensus of understanding, the Church developed a tradition of what is permitted (or even required). Often this consensus was crystallized in creeds and confessions of faith. These statements are largely the outcome of the Church's struggles to determine the legitimate meaning of the Bible, and they are in part intended to guide the readers from generation to generation. But it is important to see that even those churches which pride themselves on not having so-called "man-made creeds" have a tradition for interpreting the Bible. This is every bit as binding as a formal creed. In either case, the modern Christian reads his Bible in the context of a tradition of interpretation, whether this is defined or not and whether this is admitted or not. Even though we may not always like the Church's consensus, we must admit that when the Church exercises this function, it continues the communal character of the Bible which emerged as a community product in the first place. There really is no such thing as private

135]

interpretation; what we do have, and must preserve, is the right of personal conviction.

For example, if someone were to assert that as
he read the Bible the Word of God commanded
him to set fire to a "heretical" church, the community of faith (and the political community as
well) would insist that this is no Word from God
at all, and that the man is not to be honored as
a prophet or mystic but to be treated in a mental
hospital. These institutions have many patients
who claim to have heard the Word of God while
reading the Bible. They are hospitalized because
the Church has learned what cannot be tolerated
in the name of God's Word.

One function of the historical-critical method
is to provide help in setting the limits of permissible interpretation. For instance, the Church of
Christ, a fundamentalist group strong in Tennessee, Kentucky, Arkansas, and Texas, rejects organ
and piano music in worship because there is no
warrant for it in the New Testament. If this group
were to take the historical-critical method seriously, they would see that although this is true,
the silence is largely accidental and irrelevant.

The Church's role in guiding the understanding of the Bible has been emphasized especially
in the Roman Catholic Church. Here an infallible Church guarantees what the Bible may mean.
Protestantism has rejected the infallible Church,
and some have not been afraid to stake their case
on an infallible Book, implying that they have
an unambiguous interpretation equally infallible.
Both forms of authoritarianism must be set aside,

even though this means living without the security these positions offer. But security does not determine validity.

Moreover, we must not bind the Spirit of God to the Church, Catholic or Protestant. Whenever the Spirit is incarcerated in a particular Church, it becomes a sect. This is why the Roman Church is as sectarian as it is catholic. Since the Spirit of God is free we must always reckon with the possibility that the Spirit will speak a Word which will undermine the particular position of a church. This was the issue when Martin Luther stood unafraid against the full weight of tradition and dogma, and in the name of God's Word insisted that the Church was wrong. Protestantism dare not turn its back on such a constant possibility without ceasing to be Protestant. The community that takes seriously the authority of the Spirit speaking through the Bible always exists under the threat of reformation. The traditionalist who believes the Spirit has already had his say (except to perpetuate the tradition) will always view this possibility as the threat of anarchy. This should not surprise us, for the greatest danger to the security of the Church has never come from the hostility of men but from the free Spirit of God.

• Finally, we must not overlook the pragmatic test for the validity of the encounter with God. An important standard for judging whether the encounter was valid is the quality of life and action it produces. Paul found this an important criterion, for he had to contend with all sorts of claims made in the name of religious experience (I Corinthians 12-14). His basic principle was "Let all things be done for edification" (I Corinthians 14:26). That is, the overarching goal must always be constructive, the development of a community of faith where genuine concern (or love) is the norm (I Corinthians 13). In the same way, we must insist that genuine encounters with God have constructive consequences. We remember, of course, that what is constructive depends on the situation just as what is health promoting depends on the patient. In both cases, constructive results may call for radical surgery.

Where the community recognizes the constructive character of what is claimed in the name of an encounter with God, it believes a man's confession that God spoke to him and that he heard. When the Church admits this it also says, in effect, that it will listen seriously to what the man now has to say. This is one reason that the Church ordains ministers. The danger is that the Church may think the minister hears the Word simply because he is ordained, when it is really the other way around. The Word of God may speak to anyone who reads the Bible. This is an inescapable risk; it is also an irreducible promise.

THE READER
IN DIALOGUE

I F WE GRANT THAT THE BIBLE may become the Word of God, we still want to know how to read it as such. Without in the least subtracting from our assertion that no recipe exists for concocting encounters with God, it is still true that there is a way of reading the Bible which is appropriate to its character as the potential Word of God.

Obviously, the Bible may be read profitably in other ways. For one thing, it can be read simply as good literature. Portions of it have great literary merit, such as the Joseph saga in Genesis, selected Psalms, Job (still as good as *J. B.*), poems of Isaiah, sections of Paul's letters, or important visions in the Revelation to John. It is unfortunate that many people who read the Bible to buttress Christian doctrines seldom see the artistry of it. Not all the Bible is great literature, and the Bible is more than a literary monument; still, an appreciation of its literary merits is in order.

Another way of reading the Bible is for historical reconstruction of ancient cultures, ideas, or religions. Until the modern archeologist provided clay tablets, inscriptions, and artifacts, the Bible was the major historical source for important aspects of the ancient world. It is still a valuable source for the study of the ancient Near East; for Israelite history, it remains indispensable.

But our major concern in this chapter is to sketch the mode of reading the Bible which is appropriate to its character and to its role as the vehicle for God's Word.

How Shall I Listen for the Word?

• The art of listening is the most important part of reading the Bible.

It is not easy to listen to the Bible. Much of this essay has dealt with the cultural problems connected with our listening. But the difficulty lies deeper than our cultural context—it is the inner inertia of the reader. For one thing, people commonly avoid strenuous reading. *Life* Magazine has been so successful because it purveys information painlessly and casually. Even though the American Bible Society has published the New Testament with striking photographs so as to create a sort of *Life* Magazine format, the text still cannot be skimmed if one wants to listen. Because reading it attentively requires a certain amount of discipline, one obstacle to listening to the Bible is the sludge that has accumulated in our minds.

Students of Paul's letter to the Romans are constantly amazed that he assumed a congregation could endure such a sustained argument. (It was to be read publicly.) Every minister who reads Romans from today's pulpit knows that even ten verses are an effective tranquilizer for a cushioned congregation. Many serious readers might be willing to put up with a few minutes of listening-reading at a time, but few would be prepared to listen to Paul's entire argument in the epistle. As a matter of fact, many students in theological seminaries have never read even a single Gospel through at one sitting. Our inertia, then, hinders us also from reading a biblical document as a whole.

As trained counselors know, we do not readily listen to another person, for genuine listening requires skill and disciplined effort. Listening to an author is equally demanding. To be patient with the writer, to hear him out, is not easy. Our tendency is to draw premature conclusions, to think we know in advance what it is all about.

• How, then, shall we read the Bible so as to listen to it? To begin with, genuine listening requires paying close attention to the text. The entire battery of tools in the historical-critical kit has been developed to help the reader listen to the Bible accurately. These tools are not peculiarly biblical tools, but are common to all reading in depth. No serious reader wants to unplug his critical faculties when he picks up the Bible; therefore he realizes that some sort of historical knowledge is necessary to hear what the text says. It is a tragedy that so much of the Church's effort to educate has been a short-circuited moral-

141]

izing. Such Bible study usually takes the form of reading the text and leaping immediately to "what it means for us." This is a fundamentally important question, but the answer can scarcely come with any force if no one cares what the passage was supposed to mean in the first place.

• But we must go beyond historical orientation, for knowing the text's original purpose may not get the reader to the heart of the matter. The inner core of meaning opens up when one stops taking the text for granted and begins to ask *why* it says what it does. For example, let us assume we understand that the small state of Judah was threatened by an invasion by Syria and North Israel in the eighth century B.C. Knowing this does not keep us from being amazed that Isaiah insisted that the king will exercise his responsibilitiy not by making astute preparations to defend the country but simply by clinging to the conviction that God will make such preparation unnecessary (Isaiah 7:1-9). A nation which honored a World War II chaplain for shouting "Praise the Lord and pass the ammunition" finds it hard to understand a prophet who says "Praise the Lord and skip the ammunition."

In fact, Isaiah appears increasingly incredible to us. Hence we American readers must ask for an explanation not only of the situation but of what he said. Without this we shall not really hear what he had to say, let alone what he might have to say now. Our deeper understanding of the Bible begins when we see *why* it says what it does as well as when or how it said it.

Paul provides another example. He carried on a vigorous argument over the problem of religion as Law. In one particularly terse passage (Galatians 2:15f.) he says in effect that we know a person is not set in right relation ("justified") with God by doing what God commands ("by the works of the law") but only by a genuine commitment to what God achieved and promises in Jesus ("through faith in Jesus Christ"). To understand what he is talking about, one needs to know something of the issue at stake in the whole letter, the problems in the Galatian churches to which it is sent, the peculiar meanings words like "law" have for Paul, and similar matters of historical understanding. But beyond this, the reader who really wants to hear what Paul is saying must penetrate the words to the issue: is a right relation to God established by doing the will of God? Paul says "No!" The reader who wants to hear Paul must ask him why he says this. *The reader must press the writer to yield the rationale of his statements.*

In Paul's case, the argument runs something like this. Paul sees no salvation on the road of achievement; he had tried it and failed. By his own estimate he had been a zealous, blameless Jew (Philippians 3:4-6). Yet this whole achievement of a religious man was turned into trash (Paul's own word) when he realized that in the name of God he was trying to root out the Church, for Paul had been its first real persecutor (Galatians 1:13-16). Paul's zeal for Judaism demanded that the Church and its preposterous claim about

143]

Jesus be destroyed. Then in a moment of crisis, Paul saw the risen Jesus as Lord. Now he discovered that what had led him to oppose the Church and the Messiah was precisely his religious devotion. He had been caught red-handed, trying to destroy the work of God in the name of God. Thus Paul's own life showed the basic bankruptcy of a self-achieved, self-sustained relation to God. Paul does not say all this in so many words but it can be readily inferred from what he does say. Paul repeatedly insists that no one can establish a right relation to God. In fact, he says God's basic intent was to make men aware that they must depend on God alone for such a relationship (Romans 3:19f.).

Summarizing Paul's rationale shows how important it is for the reader to question the writer for the inner meaning of the text. The reader should bring relentless pressure to bear on the text until the underlying point is clear. Naturally, not every reader sees the same thing. But this does not excuse anyone from asking Paul the basic questions. The reader must demand that the text make sense. Otherwise, he will not be a listener at all, but only an observer without real understanding, like a Russian watching his first baseball game without an interpreter. But when the reader begins to press the text for its underlying meaning, for the logic of its assertions, then he begins to move from his observation post to a listening post. Then the excitement of hearing the Bible is at hand.

What If I Don't Agree?

• If the reader has penetrated the Bible to the point where he sees both what the text says and its rationale in saying it, then he stands at a decisive juncture. Several possibilities are now open and between them he must choose.

The simplest alternative is to be satisfied with historical understanding of what the author said. That is, the reader's purpose is achieved when he reaches adequate comprehension. This is a legitimate goal, whether one is reading a Kafka novel, the Dead Sea Scrolls, or the Gospel of John. But if the reader still wants the Bible to be Scripture for him, then a further step is in order.

This second step may be in one of two directions. It may be taken in the direction of the fundamentalist who believes he must accept what the Bible says, regardless of the consequences. For him there can be no disagreement with the Bible. Even if at some points his credulity is stretched to the breaking point, he accepts what he finds because he finds it in the Bible.

But the second step may be taken in another direction, one more appropriate to the kind of Bible we have been talking about. This step engages the reader in *a dialogue with the Bible*. That is, he begins to question it, even argue with it. Here it is not simply a matter of pressing the text for a clearer understanding of what it really means. It is really a matter of questioning whether what the text says is really true.

145]

Let us return to Paul again. Engaging the Bible in a dialogue means asking Paul directly, "Is it really true that man can do nothing to earn his salvation? Does not salvation consist of doing the will of God? Do you really mean that even 'a good Christian life' will not be enough to establish a right relation to God?" When the reader asks this kind of question, he begins to see that in writing to the Galatians Paul rejected the ultimate adequacy of every form of religious achievement, not simply that of Judaism. When this arrow finds its bull's-eye in the reader, then he finds that the gap of nineteen centuries separating him from the first readers is actually closed. Now he finds that Paul is arguing not only with the Galatians but with every man, with the reader himself. Despite our words of adulation for Paul, we seldom can afford to believe him, because we resist such a radical way of understanding our dependence on God. And so the issue is joined again, as it has been whenever Paul has begun to make his point.

When the Bible is read this way, it is no longer a casual, pious, devotional exercise in which one bolsters his preconceptions. Reading the Bible so as to hear it and respond to it can be a struggle in which the stakes are as high as life and death because the issue is man's relation to God. Since the dialogue drives the reader to an intensive (shall we say "existential"?) participation in the issue behind the text, this is the most appropriate way to read the Bible as the potential Word of God.

• Since this dialogical relation to the Bible is so important, we should see five aspects of the dialogue in closer detail. (a) The dialogue is not only permissible but mandatory. Some people may shrink from the possibility of talking back to the Bible. But they overlook the fact that this is one of the ways in which the Bible becomes a Word which confronts the reader at his deepest level. A serious dialogue with the Bible is required by the fact that God may speak to the reader more directly in this way. Unfortunately, most Bible reading is listless and lifeless because the readers are too relaxed to think sharply, too pious to argue cogently, too concerned merely to be inspired for the Word of God to accost them. No doubt, the divine Thou can slash through such dullness, but the reader ought not dare him to do it by reading the Bible in lethargy. But reading the Bible with one's energies committed to a genuine response, be it "Yes" or "No," can be electrifying.

(b) Genuine dialogue requires equal partners. It may be even more offensive to think of oneself as an equal partner with the Bible. One must respect such a stance if it stems from deep reverence for the Scripture. But it may also be simply a shield to avoid the demands of strenuous reading and probing. In any case, we talk about equal partners not to demote the Bible but to demote the reader. One who is armed with historical knowledge may silently slip into the role of a superior modern man who condescendingly reads ancient religious texts. Dealing candidly with the

147]

problems raised by our modern knowledge should not foster a superiority complex with regard to the Bible.

Let us return to Paul again. We commonly assume that because we Gentiles no longer have problems with the validity of the Jewish laws and customs (like kosher food and sacred festivals) we are really bystanders watching Paul demolish the fastidiousness of the Jews. But this is not really hearing Paul at all—it is only eavesdropping. But when we realize Paul is attacking (in principle) the ultimacy of every religion, then we are summoned to a dialogue. This dialogue with Paul can proceed only if we are no more than equal partners in the conversation. This means that just as we can put fundamental questions to Paul, so Paul can put them to us. If we assume we know better than Paul, there can be no real dialogue but only shadowboxing with theological terms. Such an exercise might be interesting if we had nothing else to do, but it is basically a waste of time. In other words, there can be no dialogue unless the reader allows himself to be interrogated by the Bible, and risks being driven to the wall by it. The real danger in undertaking such a dialogue is that the Bible might win. Danger or not, there is no dialogue at all without the possibility of being converted to biblical faith.

(c) The dialogue is continuous. This does not mean that the reader lives on the precipice all the time, for no one maintains psychologically such an intensive personal involvement. But the point is rather that the issues in the Bible are never settled so completely that the dialogue can be dropped. Instead, because one's understanding of the text constantly changes (unless he becomes an intellectual fossil), and because the reader himself changes (his history affects his reading), the dialogue with the Bible should be sustained, frequently even with the same passage. Besides, there probably will be many attempts to engage in a real dialogue which will fail, either because the text was not properly understood or because the reader was not inwardly free enough to hear what it had to say. In such cases, one should return to the passage from time to time, for often a section which is opaque today becomes luminous tomorrow. In other words, such Bible reading leads to a life of dialogue.

(d) Being a participant in an ongoing dialogue makes one a member of the community of readers. This is because the dialogical involvement puts the reader in conversation with other readers as well as with the author. When the reader converses with the writer, he joins all those who have conversed with him before. Let's examine this more closely.

At this point it may be helpful to remember that when Protestants emphasize the "inner witness of the Holy Spirit," they refer to the experience in which the reader affirms that God himself has spoken to him. Calvin, whose statements have become classical in this regard, made it unmistakably clear that apart from this the words of the Bible would never be read as the Word of

God.[1] But it is not enough simply to agree with Calvin; we must show what this means in the context of our discussion.

First of all, the witness of the Spirit is a personal experience but not a completely private one. It is not esoteric or secret; rather, it is intensely personal in such a way that others can grasp what happened even though their own experiences differ. Moreover, because the witness of the Spirit is not private, it actually generates a community of the addressed, each of whom has heard the Word of God in his own way, in his own history. The witness of the Spirit does not erase individuality but affirms it by drawing together all sorts of people to share what they have heard God say to them. Consequently, we must not conclude that any one reader's insight is absolute; rather, when the historicity of the reader is kept in mind, we draw the opposite conclusion—the witness of the Spirit points to the fact that others have been addressed also. By sharing what each has heard in the midst of his own history, one stretches his understanding to include insights

[1] Calvin's famous passage is in his *Institutes of the Christian Religion*, Book I, Ch. 7, Par. 4: "For as God alone is a fit witness of himself in his Word, so also the Word will not find acceptance in men's hearts before it is sealed by the inward testimony of the Spirit. The same Spirit, therefore, who has spoken through the mouths of the prophets must penetrate into our hearts to persuade us that they faithfully proclaimed what had been divinely commanded." Quoted from the translation by F. L. Battles in *The Library of Christian Classics*, Vol. XX, John T. McNeill, ed. (Philadelphia: The Westminster Press, 1960), p. 79.

not available otherwise. Thus one must not use the idea of the witness of the Spirit to make oneself an absolute authority with heaven-sent insights; rather, one should use it to prevent unwarranted self-confidence. The witness of the Spirit is not a private religious experience but a personal one for the sake of the community. In this light it is instructive to read Paul's comments on the variety of results which the one divine Spirit elicits in a given group (I Corinthians 12-14).

Moreover, it is important to remember that this community is not restricted to one's contemporaries, but includes the whole readership of the Bible from the very beginning. Our understanding may be enriched more by Luther or Augustine than by the latest commentary. The creeds contain the phrase "the communion of the saints." In our context, this means that the readers are related to one another not only at a given point in time but across the centuries as well. Moreover, the phrase also means that the readers are engaged in reciprocal probing and sharing. Without this dialogue the communion of the saints readily degenerates into the conformity of the stultified.

(e) The historical-critical method is an important factor in the life of dialogue. At first glance, one might infer that since the validity of the Bible hinges on meeting God, and since this is not controllable, the historical-critical enterprise is beside the point. After all, it may be argued, if God can meet you as you read, what difference does it make whether you understand what the author intended to say?

Such an appealing argument cannot be accepted. Meeting God is not an experience without content, without understanding. When God says something through the Bible, hearing his Word involves understanding what the text says. Therefore scholarly work has both a negative and a positive function. Negatively, it makes certain interpretations impossible, for it insists that we listen to what the text actually says and not simply to what we think it says or ought to say. Positively, it helps us to hear what the writer wants to say; in fact, this is the only real justification for the whole discipline.

Emphasizing the importance of scholarly study may imply that the untrained, nonprofessional reader might as well close his Bible until he becomes a historian. Actually, the opposite is the case. The real point is that the circle of students must be extended. All readers of the Bible have some kind of historical understanding of it, even if it is exceedingly rudimentary. The question is whether they are willing to give this elemental grasp significant depth and precision. The reader who thinks he does not need to study because he listens only to God's Word is irresponsible or arrogant (or both) because no one has a right to expect the divine Word to address a reader who thinks getting ready to hear is unimportant. If the Bible is to be our Scripture, it is worth reading properly.

TWO EXAMPLES
OF DIALOGUE

Oᴜʀ ᴅɪsᴄᴜssɪᴏɴ ᴡɪʟʟ ʙᴇᴄᴏᴍᴇ more concrete when we turn to two issues, science and ethics. They readily illustrate what we have been saying and they are areas of real concern.

What About the Bible and Science?

Standing on the threshhold of astronavigation makes us all aware of a conception of the universe long held by astronomers. No one expects the kind of battle once fought between the Church and Galileo to be waged again, but serious readers find themselves in a dilemma as they put down the newspaper to pick up the Bible. In fact, there are many readers of the newspaper who find it increasingly difficult to pick up the Bible at all. One reason is that there is an undeniable tension between what the Bible sometimes says about the universe and what we know about it today. But there is agreement as well as tension. After noting this, we shall turn to the problem of creation and then to the question of "miracles."

• First, we note four important areas in which the Bible and science agree. To begin, the Bible has a positive attitude toward the material world. The dictum of Genesis is never repudiated: "God saw that it [the world] was good." In the light of repeated efforts in Western culture to deny this, the biblical assertion is really an ally of scientific work. Second, the Bible agrees with science that the universe is intelligible to man. It does not say this in scientific terms; it prefers to say it in its own way: "The heavens declare the glory of God." This assumes that the heavens are not capricious or arbitrary but coherent and dependable, and hence intelligible. Third, the Bible sees man as part of the material world. Like science, the Bible knows that man is more than matter, but it is unmistakable in emphasizing continuity between man and the world of things and animals. He is made from the dust, and he can be described by the same word as is used for animals (Genesis 2:4-9, 18f.). Besides, "nature" will participate in the great fulfillment to come (Isaiah 35, Romans 8:18-39, Revelation 21:1-4). Fourth, the Bible sees man as sovereign over the world. The world is at his disposal, and he is fully human when he masters it. The best impact of biblical thought insists that scientific work is nothing less than a fulfillment of God's will that man should "fill the earth and subdue it . . . and have dominion over every living thing."

[154

Exploration of space is merely an extension of this.

These tersely stated points have not exhausted the positive relation between the Bible and science. Nonetheless, these underlying points of agreement may be more important than tensions over particulars. Yet, real tensions do exist, and we must face them.

• We begin by asking how the Bible views the world. To generalize what this diverse literature says about the world is to commit the crime of distortion. Nevertheless, a caricature may highlight important features better than a sharp photograph. This is the risk we take.

(a) Basically, the Bible does not want to provide information about the universe, though it contains ancient knowledge. In fact, documents which were interested in such information, such as Enoch, were rejected from the Bible. Rather, the Bible is concerned with the universe primarily as it bears on the central concern—the meaning of human life. The Bible is not interested in disclosing the structure or the size of the cosmos. In the light of the battles which have been fought over the Bible and science, perhaps this omission should be seen as an act of Providence.

(b) The biblical conceptions of the universe reflect the historicity of the Bible. Consequently, the Bible has a double relation to the ideas of the universe: it accepted the ideas of the time and it modified them. Both elements must be seen.

The Bible shares the world view with its neighbors. Since the Bible was written over a span of thirty generations living in three cultures, there is no single world view but several. The earliest is apparently the Babylonian and the latest the Hellenistic, built on earlier foundations. None of these are our world views. The fundamental difference is that we have discarded the idea of how the cosmos is structured (three floors, Hell or Hades, earth, heaven) and insist that the only means of knowing about this universe is by scientific study. Our cosmos has no angels, demons, or other supraterrestrial beings with whom we must contend. Though science-fiction deals with Martians, we do not regard these as having such a control of the world that we must reckon with them religiously. Even if life on Mars should prove to be superior to ours, this would not be scientific confirmation of the Bible's angels and archangels.

As a matter of fact, there have been many such attempts to harmonize the Bible and science by making the Bible anticipate what science discovers. A famous attempt was trying to squeeze the geological periods of the earth's history into the six days of creation; another is the attempt to identify the Christmas star with a planet or comet. Such efforts are a waste of time and should be given up, for they mock both science and the Bible.

Because the Bible shares its ideas about the world with the eras in which it was written, there can be no denying a tension between some things the Bible says and what we know of the world.

In fact, the more we know about both the Bible and the world, the greater becomes the gulf between science and Scripture at certain points. This is not because science is antireligious but because the gulf that separates our knowledge of the world from that of ancient times is widening. Because the Bible thinks of the world in terms of its own, the gap is growing. In other words, it is the historicity of both the Bible and the modern reader which separates them.

(c) The Bible, however, did not simply borrow ideas of the world from surrounding cultures, but modified what it used. That is, it adapted the ideas it adopted. We may illustrate this with Genesis and Colossians, the former dealing with creation, the latter with salvation.

Important features of the creation story are shared with the Babylonian creation myth. When the Mesopotamian material was first found, many thought the Bible offered simply a truncated version edited for Hebrew readers. Closer study has corrected this. There are real parallels and influences which cannot be denied. But important differences outweigh similarities. For one thing, the Babylonian account says the world resulted from a battle among the gods; the loser was halved like a fillet and made into earth and sky while from her blood man was created. In contrast, Genesis refuses to speculate about what God was doing before he created the world; moreover, it has no room for any conflict because the story shows God as the absolute master of the situation. Besides, in Genesis man is made

157]

from dust instead of being a blood relative of the gods. Thus, though doubtless the Babylonian myth lies in the background (this is clearer in the Hebrew text), the biblical writers so completely transformed it that it could never be recovered from the text of Genesis alone.

Paul's letter to the Colossians comes from the more sophisticated Greco-Roman world. For centuries men believed that stars and planets were the abodes of heavenly beings which must be respected. After Alexander's conquests bequeathed Greek culture to the world (much like the recent Americanization of half the globe), the accumulated observations of the astrologers were correlated with mathematical knowledge. The result was revolutionary, for now it was possible to calculate the relationships between heavenly powers and beings. Here was a genuinely scientific basis for religion! The Stoics used the new knowledge to exhort men to integrate their lives to the rhythm of the cosmos, for they said man was a constituent part of this vast organism. Dualists, on the other hand, believed that man's eternal soul was imprisoned in a temporal body. The new knowledge now meant that the stars ruled the body and that this rule could be gauged. Hence, the more precisely one calculated the movements of the heavenly world, the more efficient the cosmic penal system appeared. Salvation lay not in getting into step with the universe but in getting out of it altogether.

The letter to the Colossians presupposes this view and is not intelligible without it. The Colossian Christians apparently believed that although Jesus was the Savior, these cosmic powers needed to be dealt with in traditional ways—by observing special days and seasons and by practicing rites to show one was free from their control. Paul does not argue the basic cosmology at all. He seems to share the point of departure and says that the resurrection of Jesus broke the power of cosmic forces: "He disarmed the principalities and powers [one of Paul's phrases for them] and made a public example of them, triumphing over them in him" (Colossians 2:15). Therefore, Paul argued, all efforts to come to terms with them were really repudiating the resurrection.

Genesis and Colossians show how contemporary ideas affect what the Bible says. The writers are not deliberately choosing a mode of discourse the way a printer selects a kind of type: rather, they shared these views themselves. But they also heard something distinctive. In other words, just as the biblical writers are indebted to the tradition of Israel's history, so they are indebted to their age for what they say or assume about the world. Moreover, just as they say something creative within their tradition, so they say something new about the world, and they do so without pretending to offer a divinely revealed science. Strictly speaking, there is no such thing as "Christian science" because there is no such thing as Christian nature.

(d) The Bible's main concern with nature is to see it as creation. Only the most indispensable matters can be touched here. First, the idea of

159]

creation does not depend on a particular theory of the world's origin. Therefore it is useless as a criterion for deciding whether one thinks the universe originated by condensation or by explosion. In such matters we must follow scientific evidence by scientific method. The biblical conviction of creation says nothing about the process at all; it is concerned solely with the meaning of what exists.

Second, the Bible insists that the phenomenal world is not eternal but had a starting point. The Bible nowhere says explicitly what the Church later said—that the world was created from nothing, *ex nihilo*.[1] But it implies this and, when the question was asked, it was made explicit. The Church made the matter clear because it was forced to choose between clear alternatives. Some (Marcion for instance) said that there were two gods, one of whom created this evil world as his domain. Others said matter was really eternal and the Creator was only an Artificer, a divine Shaper of things which already existed. Others said the world evolved downward from God through a series of links in a descending chain of

[1] One of the books of the Apocrypha, however, says virtually the same thing: "God did not make them [things in heaven or earth] out of things that existed." The sentence can also be translated, "God made them out of things that did not exist" (II Maccabees 7:28). Although this book is not part of the Protestant Bible, it does show that in a setting in which matter is held to be virtually eternal, the biblical understanding of God as Creator leads naturally to a *creatio ex nihilo* position since the alternative compromises the sovereignty of God over nature.

being. In this view, existence degenerated as it descended; earth and man were near the bottom of the ladder. Over against all these views, the Church picked up the theme of Genesis—that prior to the cosmos there was only God, and that the universe depends immediately on him and not on some intermediary demigod. The Church was not trying to provide scientific answers but to understand man's relation to the world and to God. Saying the universe began when God deliberately created it from nothing at all, is not a scientific assertion but a theological conviction about how God, man, and the world are related.

In the third place, we note two important consequences of the idea of creation. One is that everything is radically and totally contingent on a Source beyond the cosmos. Neither man nor nature are autonomous or self-explanatory. With this contingency goes the fact that man is responsible to God. Here again we see the Bible's intent: not a scientific report but a basis for the moral character of man. The Bible does not claim that moral laws are built into the universe, as Stoics said, but it does insist that man is a moral being because he is created in the image of a moral God. The doctrine of creation also implies that man is responsible to God alone. Since he is not the outcome of a cosmic tug-of-war, he owes ultimate allegiance only to the Creator. The Devil has no place in the story of creation; the Bible says he does his work afterward. In the Bible, moreover, the Devil always operates on usurped authority. Consequently, neither nature nor any other power in the cosmos is to be worshiped. The real intent of creation-theology is to insist *that nothing phenomenal is ultimate, that everything phenomenal is relative, that it is relative to God alone.* Biblical monotheism is not speculation about the numerical character of God but the conviction that only he is God.

The concept of creation, then, does not conflict with scientific theories, but it may conflict basically with the way a scientist views the world which he studies. The idea of creation does not control experiments, but it summons the experimenter to understand himself as a creature studying other creatures.

• The most common area of difficulty is the miracles. Miracles have dominated so many discussions of science and the Bible because a wrong assumption has reigned—that the authority of the Bible stands or falls with the miracle stories. Defenders of the Bible still put it this way, "If I can't believe everything in the Bible, how can I believe anything?" Usually the inference is that one must therefore swallow it whole. This essay tries to show another way because such an argument is really a blind alley. On the other hand, debunkers have often claimed more than they knew when they ruled out all reports of the miraculous. The fate of the healing stories in Jesus' ministry illustrates this. Psychosomatic healing has made many stories credible again. Not every story is now rehabilitated, but the problem has been reshaped. Because the miracle question is most pressing in the study of Jesus, we limit the discussion to these stories.

Rather than beginning by sorting the stories into two piles, the credible and the incredible, it is better to ask what each story was intended to convey. Beginning here also helps to avoid rationalizing the stories—that is, finding rational, respectable, ordinary reasons for stories about the unusual and irrational. The rationalist says that Jesus did not feed 5,000 people with five loaves and two fish (Mark 8:1-10), but actually induced each person to share his hidden biscuit with his neighbor. Fundamentalists have always repudiated this procedure, and rightly, for it tries to make the stories true by rewriting them. When we begin by asking what the story intended to convey, we temporarily postpone the question, "What really happened?" This is a valid question, but it is not the place to begin.

Beginning with the intent of the story helps us to see that the Bible actually has no concept of "miracle" at all. Having no idea of natural law, it does not look on the stories as reports of how the laws of nature were momentarily suspended. The Bible's own terms for these events is "mighty acts of God" or "signs and wonders." That is, the Bible is interested in such stories because they point beyond themselves ("signs") to something more important. We are the miraclemongers, not the Bible. In fact, the Gospels report that Jesus refused to give "signs" when they were requested (Mark 8:11-13).

Moreover, the Bible does not try to prove a

theological point by appealing to the miracles. This is a clear difference between the biblical Gospels and those not in the Bible. The Gospel of James, for instance, tries to prove the Virgin Birth of Jesus by reporting that a midwife inspected Mary.[2] It is amazing that people continue to say the miracles prove the divinity of Jesus when the New Testament Gospels report the opposite—that in his own lifetime they proved nothing at all, and that some observers concluded his power was not divine but demonic (Mark 3:20-33). Even if one could prove beyond a doubt that the miracle stories are literally true, this would prove nothing at all except that these things happened.

John's Gospel, however, contains passages which suggest that miracles do show who Jesus was (for example, 2:11, 5:36, 7:31). But when these statements are seen in the light of the whole document, it is apparent that John sees the ambiguity of the miracles just as clearly as do the others. In fact, the ambiguity is actually sharp-

[2] Gospel of James, Ch. 19. See M.R. James, *The Apocryphal New Testament, op. cit.,* p. 46. The Gospel of Thomas (not the one recently discovered in Egypt) reports the childhood of Jesus in a similar vein—a series of miraculous events such as making twelve clay pigeons fly or taking over the first grade at school to lecture on mystical meanings of the alphabet. The apocryphal acts of various apostles report the same sort of stories, such as John's ordering the bedbugs out of the bed in a third-class inn and then permitting them to return in the morning after he had slept. Reading the apocryphal miracle stories will show how really reticent the biblical accounts are.

ened. John reports that "many believed in his name when they saw his signs which he did; but Jesus did not trust himself to them. . ." (John 2:23). Moreover, whenever Jesus discloses himself in this Gospel, the usual response is an argument or a misunderstanding (for instance, John 9:13-34). That is, the wondrous deeds of Jesus are reported in such a way that the believer sees them as manifestations of Jesus' mission but the nonbeliever is offended. To make this perfectly clear, John reports that once a voice spoke to Jesus from heaven; the crowd, however, argued whether this was an angel or thunder (John 12:27-30). This Gospel, then, has little confidence in the persuasive power of the miraculous.

In short, the Bible knows that to the believer the miracles may bring corroboration, but to him who does not believe, they are only reports of the bizarre and the incredible.

Following the intent of the stories further leads us to distinguish between the Gospel stories about Jesus' healings and the stories which glorify Jesus himself, like his walking on water. Many of the healing stories are quite credible in the light of our knowledge of neuroses, especially as symptoms of guilt. But many stories in the latter category are the kind of evidence Jesus himself rejected—signs to demonstrate his power (for example, Mark 8:11-13). Consequently, the healing stories have a greater degree of reliability. However, they should not be read as case histories but as popular stories about real healings.

Our main problem is with the second group,

165]

the stories which are told to present the power of Jesus. Honesty requires us to admit that our total knowledge of the world leads us to insist that the only time axe heads float (II Kings 6:1-7) or people walk on water (Mark 6:47-52) is when it is frozen. When we read such stories we can conclude that either the stories are not reports of real events or that our physics does not apply to Jesus and the Bible. As far as Jesus is concerned, the Church has always insisted that anyone who says Jesus is exempt from the rules is a heretic because he undermines the full humanity of Jesus. It is better, then, to take the former alternative.

In fact, were such stories not in the Bible we should not hesitate at all. If we should read that Mohammed walked across the Red Sea we should conclude that this is a pious Islamic invention. But we cannot have one standard for stories in the Bible and another for stories outside it. In matters of this kind we cannot believe something simply because it is in the Bible. At first glance, believing the incredible simply because it is biblical may look like real faithfulness to the Scripture; on second glance, however, it really makes the Bible irrelevant because it makes it stand outside life as we know it. Nonetheless, such stories are part of the Bible which is our Scripture. If we cannot take them as accounts of real events, what can we do with them?

Such stories should neither be rationalized nor discarded completely. For one thing, this would

[166

make it difficult to listen to the writers for whom the stories are important. Beyond this, since the Bible is not miracle-mad, we must ask whether we have correctly understood the intent of the story. Frequently, it is rewarding to listen again. For example, the story of Jesus walking on water was told as a symbol to convey the presence of Jesus with his people in the night of despair. To read it simply as an account of how Jesus suspended or defied the law of floating bodies is to miss the point. Similarly, the story of how Jesus fed the thousands is not concerned primarily to show how Jesus could set up a soup kitchen in the wilderness: rather, it is told to show how the whole Church can be fed with the bread Jesus blessed—the bread of the Lord's Supper.

Clearly, there is a danger of arbitrarily allegorizing whatever is objectionable so that new spiritual meanings emerge everywhere. This danger cannot be avoided. It can, however, be minimized by listening closely to what the author is trying to say. Even so, it is clear that not every story will convey such a deeper meaning. In this case, we may simply shake our heads and say, "I'm sorry, but I can't follow you here." Nothing is gained by pretending to believe something we really don't.

In conclusion, the issue of science and the Bible provides a clear occasion for the reader to carry on a dialogue with the Bible. The tensions between our science and certain biblical statements cannot be handled by a pious statement that there can be no conflict between science and the Bible because God is responsible for both.[3] Instead, the reader will maintain his integrity if he learns he need not feel guilty if, after questioning the Bible for what it says and implies about the universe, he concludes that our scientific data are more reliable. At the same time, the dialogue will be maintained if the reader allows the Bible to maintain its integrity also. This means not twisting it so as to make it keep up to date with our science, but allowing it to keep its historicity. Even more, it means allowing the fundamental concern of the Bible to question the reader, to compel him to decide whether or not he will understand himself as a creature whose existence is totally dependent on One who transcends everything. When the Bible elicits a fundamental decision on this issue, its authority will be demonstrated.

How Is the Bible Relevant for Ethics?

There is also a tension between the Bible and the things we do every day. For example, if the specific prohibitions and commands in the Bible were to be enforced, men would stop shaving

[3] Such a statement was made by Ulric Jelinek: "Nature and the Bible must say the same thing because God wrote them both. If there is any conflict in your mind, you will find that there is something wrong either with the interpretation or the observation of the facts. The Bible is written in the language of the common man in the culture of the day, and yet, when it speaks about science, it is scientifically correct." This is a typical fundamentalist position. Ulric Jelinek, "A Scientist Contemplates the Universe and Its Creator," *The Collegiate Challenge*, Oct., 1961, p. 6.

and women would give up permanents and jewelry (Leviticus 19:27, I Corinthians 11:2-16, I Timothy 2:9); no clothes would contain mixed fibers (Deuteronomy 22:11); no farmer could develop hybrids or cross-breed his stock (Leviticus 19:19); meals would no longer include pork, crabs, lobsters, rabbits (Leviticus 11); banks could charge interest on loans made only to foreigners (Deuteronomy 23:19f.) and any unpaid loans to fellow citizens would be canceled every seventh year (Deuteronomy 15:1-3); juvenile delinquents would be executed (Deuteronomy 21:18-22); and illegitimate children would be ostracized (Deuteronomy 23:2).

But instead of cataloguing such points, we are more concerned to discuss basic areas of life where the Bible stands in tension with our prevailing mores and assumptions.

• We begin with the relation of the Bible to democracy. The Bible knows nothing about it; it is thoroughly theocratic. The Bible believes that God is the absolute sovereign, and he is often called "king" (for instance, I Samuel 8:1-9, Psalm 99, Isaiah 6:1-4). The Old Testament gets no closer to democracy than insisting that the Israelite king be responsible to God and to his fellow Israelites. This "democratic vein" has nothing to do with the worth of every person but with the obligation to be faithful to a brother Israelite. The New Testament does not get even this far, since it ignores political theory and pushes the political character of Jesus' Messiahship into the background or into heaven ("My kingdom is not of this world," John 18:36). The genuinely biblical idea of government does not point to modern democratic society but to Brigham Young and the theocracy of the Mormons. Besides, when the Bible speaks of the future, it talks about the "kingdom of God" (better translated "kingship"). There is no thought of participating in the processes of government in God's kingdom. If God has an agent it is the Messiah; he is not elected by men but sent by God. In short, one simply cannot say that the Bible teaches democracy as a way of life.

The New Testament intensifies the problem. It admonishes believers to pay taxes, obey the law, honor the emperor, and be solid citizens (see Mark 12:13-17, Romans 13:1-5, I Peter 2:13-17), but it never reports an apostle engaged in public affairs other than preaching. Joseph Klausner, the Jewish scholar who wrote an important study of Jesus, pointed out that such "irresponsibility" is traceable to Jesus himself, for he showed no concern for the structure of society [4]; in fact, Jesus said he came to disrupt a fundamental institution—the family (Matthew 10:34-39). The main stream of the Mennonite tradition has insisted that the Christian should not participate in government at all, either in war or in voting. In a sense, this view has the weight of the New Testament pattern behind it. What, then,

[4] Joseph Klausner, *Jesus of Nazareth*, Herbert Danby, tr. (New York: The Macmillan Company, 1925), pp. 373ff.

is the authority of the Bible for a society based on wide participation in public affairs?

A second area in which we have problems with the Bible is that of family life, the role of women, attitudes toward sex and divorce. The Bible has exercised real authority in such matters. Until recently, the Church did not tolerate divorce because the New Testament forbids it.[5] Similarly, Paul's command that women remain silent in church (I Corinthians 14:33b-36) has made ordaining women impossible until recently.

A third sensitive area is race relations. The end of Caucasian domination is as irreversible as it is incontestable. No government today can withstand the pressure for equality for all. This is long

---

[5] Actually, the statements are not altogether uniform. According to Mark 10:1-12, Jesus went beyond the Old Testament status of divorce (Deuteronomy 24:1-4) by prohibiting it altogether as a violation of God's primary intent in creation. Mark reports that the disciples questioned Jesus about such a radical ruling, and Matthew reports the same pronouncement with a significant change —no divorce except for unchastity (Matthew 19:1-12). Paul's rejection of divorce (I Corinthians 7) is motivated largely by his concern to prevent Christianity from becoming a wedge between a Christian husband and his non-Christian wife. All his statements on the subject must also be gauged in the light of his keen expectation that the end of the entire fabric of society was as we know it just around the corner; in such a situation, he did not want people to become embroiled in problems which had only momentary significance. As it became clear that society would continue far beyond anything Paul (or anyone else in the New Testament) really expected, it also became evident that Paul's statements must be rethought. In certain particulars Paul himself recognized that he was improvising without explicit authority from Jesus' words (I Corinthians 7:10, 12, 25, 40).

overdue. Nonetheless, there are real tensions between this pressure and parts of the Bible.

Doubtless some passages in the Bible call for a kind of segregation of the Jews. Though its advocate, Ezra, did not insist on "Compounds for Canaanites" he certainly did require Jewish *apartheid* (Ezra 2:59-63, 9:1-15). Even more famous is the passage in Genesis which appears to support the subjugation of the Africans (Genesis 9:25-27). Several years ago, this was quoted to buttress segregation. This pernicious misinterpretation overlooked the fact that the alleged curse on the Negro was spoken by Noah when he emerged from a drunken stupor in which he had lain naked in his tent. Those who used this to support segregation were claiming that what Noah muttered in a hangover was the eternal Word of God on the subject!

Perhaps more fundamental to the tension is the fact that basically the Bible does not advocate social reconstruction as such. The prophets indeed denounce injustice, but they do not advocate a program of social change in general. The New Testament accepts slavery and does not seek to change this institution or any other. In fact, Paul rejects using Christianity as a springboard for changing one's status in society (I Corinthians 7:17-24). What, then, is the authority of the Bible in our day when the whole world is in the throes of some kind of revolution?

• Instead of discussing each point raised in detail, we shall deal with the authority of the Bible in social ethics by emphasizing two points.

The first is that we must constantly keep in mind the historicity of the Bible. This means that the Bible shares the social attitudes and assumptions of its era just as it does the science of the age. Thus the Bible takes slavery for granted but seeks to regulate the treatment of slaves (Exodus 21, Ephesians 6:5-9). Likewise, it assumes women are subordinate (I Corinthians 11:2-16, I Peter 3:1-7) and that the monarch is supreme.

Bearing in mind the historicity of the Bible also helps us to see the impact particular circumstances have on what is said on ethical matters. Thus, the reason Ezra insists on semi-isolation for the Jews is that this is the only way he sees for a minority group to maintain its identity. Similarly, attention to circumstances helps us to understand the New Testament's silence on responsible action in public life. Thus, we remember that at the time there was no Jewish state in which the apostles could help to shape policy as the prophets once did (for instance, I Kings 22). The only way they could have participated was by joining the underground movement against the Romans; from this, however, they dissociated themselves (Acts 21:37-39). Moreover, the Church expected the end of history momentarily; there simply was no point in getting involved in a society which was about to be replaced. Besides, before long Christians were persecuted by the state. In such a situation, they could share in governmental activity more as lion fodder or as living torches for Nero's garden parties.

Consequently, simply quoting "what the Bible

says" on social matters (or does not say) is of interest but need not be decisive. The problems which emerge in our kind of society are not solved by quoting what the Bible said to problems of another kind of society. In fact, the more specifically the biblical statements address the ethical problems of its time, the less relevant they may be today. The regulations with which we began this discussion illustrate this amply. Nowhere is the historicity of the Bible more evident than in its ethics.

The second thing which must be emphasized is that the historicity of the ethical commands of the Bible does not make the Bible irrelevant, because more important than explicit regulations are the underlying assumptions. As in matters touching science, so in ethical problems the significant impact of the Bible comes from under the surface. We note briefly four important assumptions.

(a) Righteousness is axiomatic. This term does not mean goodness or justice (an alternate translation) in the common sense but means a right relation to a norm. For the Bible, the norm is not a built-in moral law of the universe but the character of God. Hence the Bible insists that God requires righteousness and that religion and morality (love of God and neighbor) are inseparable. In this way, the Bible opposes the idea that God is an impersonal Power, an a-moral It. The Bible also rejects all contemporary pressure to confine religion to worship, so that the preacher will con-

[174

cern himself with getting us to heaven but will leave life on Main Street alone.

The Bible's concern for righteousness gives its own kind of support to democracy. The Bible is conducive to democracy because it sees man as a responsible sinner (both words are important) whose power must be restrained if justice is to be achieved. Implicit biblical support for democracy does not come from happy idealism about every man's worth or his capacity for sound judgment; rather, it flows from sober realism about every man's tendency to sin against his neighbor if he can get away with it. Likewise, the Bible tacitly supports democracy by holding that although government is divinely ordained neither kings nor their policies have automatic divine sanction. (James I could not have afforded to listen closely to the Bible!) Perhaps the current dissolution of democratic patterns in our industrial and urban society can be checked by shifting our ideology away from rationalism to biblical realism. At least, the Bible provides a better clue to understanding the corruption of legislators and voting habits than do John Locke and Thomas Jefferson.

(b) God's concern for righteousness becomes specific. The Bible, therefore, is more interested in particular legislation than with theories of law; it is not content to exhort the reader to be kind and honest in general but is concerned to say specifically what kindness and honesty mean. This is why the Bible contains so many commandments, dealing with the whole range of human life, from commands against murder to prohibi-

175]

tions against cooking a kid in its mother's milk. When the writers included such details they were not being picayune; rather, they expressed the conviction that God's will is specific.

The critical historian has shown that much of this legislation is shared with the ancient Near East in general; that is, the specific commands reflect the historicity of the Bible. But the underlying assumption is not nullified by this. Where the underlying assumption that God's will is specific is really seen, the reader risks similar judgments about God's specific will. Pastors who do this from the pulpit have the authority of the Bible behind them when they speak to specific problems of our time even though they may not have this authority for the actual judgments they make. In other words, the real authority of the Bible lies in rescuing Christian ethics from platitudes about goodness and love, and in summoning people to specific acts of obedience and justice.

(c) Religion and nationalism are separable in a way religion and ethics are not. At first this does not seem valid because the covenant theology interweaves the destiny of Israel with the promise of God. But the decisive point here is that gradually the Bible becomes convinced that it must distinguish between a religious understanding of Israel's fortunes and religious chauvinism. Gradually, the insight was clarified that the real destiny of Israel does not depend on the glorious existence of the Jewish state. It took the total destruction of the country in 586 B.C.

to drive the point home. It was the so-called Second Isaiah (Isaiah 40ff.) who insisted that God's real purpose would be achieved through a people whose national life had been destroyed.

This emerging conviction opposes all recent efforts to see Christianity as an arm of the State Department, or vice versa. The Bible does not oppose patriotism, but it knows that God's purposes are not tied to the fortunes of any state, nor is the existence of the Church. The Bible repudiates the notion that if Western democracy should succumb to communism, Christianity is doomed with it.

(d) For the Christian, Jesus is decisive. This may take the form of making his life and axioms the pattern for Christian ethics. When this occurs, the follower of Jesus does not woodenly imitate everything Jesus did (remain unmarried, wear sandals, live "on the road" with friends). Rather, he finds ways of allowing the pulse of Jesus' life to throb in his own situation today; that is, problems of contemporary life suggest ways the example of Jesus is to be followed. This is not so much asking, "What kind of engineer would Jesus be?" as asking, "What does the demeanor of his life compel me, an engineer, to be?"

Working out the implication of God's work in Jesus may take another, more subtle, form. Here one does not necessarily look for precedents in Jesus' life but for consequences of the Christ-event as a whole. For example, Jesus said nothing about segregation and seems to have accepted the primary place of the Jews in the purpose of

177]

God. This does not put the problems of segregation outside the scope of Jesus' meaning, however. We see this through Paul who faced an analogous situation in Antioch: Jewish Christians segregated themselves from their Gentile brethren. They had no serious objections to their becoming Christians but they saw no reason why they should worship together or, especially, eat the Lord's Supper together. Paul argued that what God achieved in Jesus was a relation which is not affected by cultural distinctions between Jew and Gentile. Therefore, when the congregation segregated the observance of the Lord's Supper, it was denying the heart of the gospel (Galatians 2). This instance shows the need to go beyond "imitating Jesus" to thinking about social problems in the light of what Jesus means, and to *making our own decisions under his impact*. This is why Christian ethics and Christian theology are so closely related.

In conclusion, the tensions between the ethos of our society and the ethical mandates in the Bible provide an important occasion for the reader to carry on his dialogue with the Bible. Whether it be the growing alliance between frustrated generals and frustrated preachers, the problems of family ethics or race relations, the reader finds himself pulled one way by our society and summoned in another direction by the Bible. Here the reader maintains his integrity by asking fundamental questions about the Bible and its meaning; he also allows the Bible to interrogate him. At some point however, he must decide which authority will be paramount for him.

      ❋   ❋   ❋

We may conclude this essay by observing that the authority of the Bible is characterized by dialogue in concentric circles. (a) The main dialogue is between the Bible and the reader. After pursuing historical understanding until one is reasonably sure he deals with the author and not with a misconception of him, the reader and the writer probe one another's convictions. The author risks being set aside by the reader; the reader risks being won over by the writer and being accosted by the divine Thou. (b) This dialogue occurs in a community of faith, whether the reader is an actual member of a church or not. A stream of interpretation guides the reader's understanding, and he is drawn into the community of interpreters. At the same time, reading the Bible dialogically and hearing the Word personally brings a dialogue with the community because the reader asks whether it has understood the Word or not. Consequently reader and community test one another, and each risks being reformed. (c) The reader hears the Word within a culture with a history. Consequently, hearing the Word elicits a critique of the culture and a review of its history in the light of the divine Word. At the same time, society and culture press the reader for the basis of his prophetic protests, and this drives him back to the Bible and the Word.

In each of these three circles, the reader is involved in a dialogue brought about and sustained by the Bible. Any concrete decision or act is, to borrow a term from physics, the resolution of these three forces. None of the partners in dialogue can claim absolute authority because historicity affects them all. Only the Word of God is absolute, and the Spirit of God enables it to work through all three. The place to learn how to recognize the Word and how to listen for it is the Bible. This is why it is still Scripture.

FOR CONTINUING
CONVERSATION

THE FOLLOWING BOOKS provide opportunity to continue discussion of a variety of matters raised in the essay. Most books in the list were written with the general reader in mind and are still in print. Because they represent a spectrum of interests and opinions they may suggest ways in which the reader can proceed on his own route to understanding and faith.

THE BIBLE IN ITS ORIGINAL SETTING

Bultmann, Rudolf, *Primitive Christianity in Its Contemporary Setting*, R.H. Fuller, tr.—Living Age Books (New York: Meridian Books, 1957).

The world's foremost New Testament scholar shows how Christianity is indebted to both Hebrew and Hellenistic cultures.

Wright, G. Ernest, *Biblical Archeology* (Philadelphia: The Westminster Press, 1961), abridged edition in paperback.

An experienced excavator and recognized interpreter of the Old Testament shows the significance of archeology for the Bible.

THE DEVELOPMENT OF THE BIBLE AS SCRIPTURE

Barclay, William, *The Making of the Bible*—Bible Guides No. 1 (Nashville: Abingdon Press, 1961).

A brief sketch of the major factors in the process.

Filson, Floyd, *Which Books Belong in the Bible?* (Philadelphia: The Westminster Press, 1957).

A discussion of problems of determining what literature shall be Scripture and of living with the decision.

MacGregor, Geddes, *The Bible in the Making* (New York: J.B. Lippincott Co., 1959).

Popular treatment of the entire process from the setting of the original writers to the modern translations.

Price, I.M., *The Ancestry of Our English Bible* (New York: Harper & Brothers, 1956—3d. ed. revised by W.A. Irwin and A.P. Wikgren).

Deals in considerable depth with the entire development of the Bible and the transmission of the documents.

INTERPRETING BIBLICAL CRITICISM

Hahn, Herbert F., *The Old Testament in Modern Research* (Philadelphia: Muhlenberg Press, 1954).

A documented survey useful for interpreting the phases of Old Testament study.

Hunter, A.M., *Interpreting the New Testament 1900-1950* (Philadelphia: The Westminster Press, 1951).

A brief survey relating a spectrum of scholars to major issues.

Marty, Martin E., ed., *New Directions in Biblical Thought*—Reflection Book (New York: Association Press, 1960).

Five essays discussing contemporary issues in biblical scholarship.

Neil, William, *The Rediscovery of the Bible* (New York: Harper & Brothers, 1954).

The first part introduces contemporary scholarship; the last sketches the Bible's content in this light.

THE FUNDAMENTALIST APPROACH TO THE BIBLE

Berkhof, L., *Principles of Biblical Interpretation* (Grand Rapids: Baker Book House, 1950).

Protestant scholasticism's elaborate apparatus for preserving the Bible's absolute authority.

Henry, C.F.H., ed., *Revelation and the Bible* (Grand Rapids: Baker Book House, 1958).

Twenty-four brief essays by sophisticated fundamentalists reflect a shift away from extreme positions taken a generation ago.

Stonehouse, N.B., and Wooley, Paul, eds., *The Infallible Word* (Philadelphia: Presbyterian Guardian Publishing Corporation, 1946).

Seven essays reflecting fairly rigid Calvinistic fundamentalism.

THE AUTHORITY OF THE BIBLE

Dodd, C.H., *The Authority of the Bible* (New York: Harper & Brothers, 1929—Torchbook reprint, 1958).

The leading British New Testament scholar surveys the Bible in terms of the kinds of authority represented by its own contents.

Knox, John, *Criticism and Faith* (Nashville, Tenn., Abingdon Press, 1952).

An important American New Testament scholar discusses the impact biblical criticism does and does not have on Christian faith.

Tillich, Paul, *Biblical Religion and the Search for Ultimate Reality* (Chicago: University of Chicago Press, 1955).

A pace-setting theologian shows how biblical faith and metaphysical thinking can be related; the book is much more important than its size suggests.

GUIDES TO THE MESSAGE OF THE BIBLE

Anderson, Bernhard, *Rediscovering the Bible* (New York: Association Press, 1951).

A well-known, competent discussion of the theological content of the Bible presented as "the forward-moving drama of God's action. . . ."

Denbeaux, Fred, *Understanding the Bible*—in Layman's Theological Library (Philadelphia: The Westminster Press, 1958).

A brief book which orients the reader to the outlook of the Bible without summarizing it so that he may read it profitably for himself.

Neil, William, *Modern Man Looks at the Bible*—Reflection Book (New York: Association Press, 1958).

A good introduction to the sweep of the Bible's contents and to its basic theological outlook.

Wright, G.E. and Fuller, R.H., *The Book of the Acts of God*— Anchor Book (Garden City, N.Y.: Doubleday & Co., 1960).

A survey of the Bible focusing on "the movement of biblical theology" from the Hebrew Exodus through the New Testament documents; also discusses the Apocrypha and Dead Sea Scrolls.

THE BIBLE AND PARTICULAR PROBLEMS

Cole, William G., *Sex and Love in the Bible* (New York: Association Press, 1959).

A "bifocal" survey of the biblical attitudes and of their contemporary relevance; the author deals with a spectrum of matters from God's love to man's incest.

Cullmann, Oscar, *The State in the New Testament* (New York: Charles Scribner's Sons, 1956).

A survey of the problems beginning with the role of the Roman government in the ministry and death of Jesus.

Gilkey, Langdon, *Maker of Heaven and Earth* (Garden City, N.Y.: Doubleday & Co., 1959.).

A theological analysis of the doctrine of creation which deals in depth with the meaning of the biblical affirmation, and the problems posed by modern science.

Tilson, Everett, *Segregation and the Bible* (Nashville,Tenn.: Abingdon Press, 1958).

A survey of the Bible showing how it undermines this custom.

HADDAM HOUSE BOOKS

Primer for Protestants	James Hastings Nichols
Youth Asks About Religion	Jack Finegan
Young Laymen—Young Church	John Oliver Nelson
The Human Venture in Sex, Love, and Marriage	Peter A. Bertocci
Science and Christian Faith	Edward LeRoy Long, Jr.
Rediscovering the Bible	Bernhard W. Anderson
The Unfolding Drama of the Bible	Bernhard W. Anderson
The Student Prayerbook	John Oliver Nelson and Others, Editors
Community of Faith	T. Ralph Morton
Politics for Christians	William Muehl
The Paradoxes of Democracy	Kermit Eby and June Greenlief
The Tragic Vision and the Christian Faith	Nathan A. Scott, Editor
Conscience on Campus	Waldo Beach
The Renewal of Hope	Howard Clark Kee
The Prophetic Voice in Modern Fiction	William R. Mueller
Christianity and Communism Today	John C. Bennett
The Christian as a Doctor	James T. Stephens and Edward LeRoy Long, Jr.
Christianity and the Scientist	Ian G. Barbour
The Art of Christian Doubt	Fred Denbeaux
The Christian as a Journalist	Richard T. Baker
As Christians Face Rival Religions	Gerald Cooke
Taking the Bible Seriously	Leander E. Keck